SERIOUS CHARGE

A Play in Three Acts

by

PHILIP KING

LONDON
SAMUEL FRENCH LIMITED

Copyright © 1955 by Philip King
© (Acting Edition) 1956 by Philip King
All Rights Reserved

SERIOUS CHARGE is fully protected under the copyright laws of the British Commonwealth, including Canada, the United States of America, and all other countries of the Copyright Union. All rights, including professional and amateur stage productions, recitation, lecturing, public reading, motion picture, radio broadcasting, television and the rights of translation into foreign languages are strictly reserved.

ISBN 978-0-573-01405-5

www.samuelfrench.co.uk

www.samuelfrench.com

FOR AMATEUR PRODUCTION ENQUIRIES

UNITED KINGDOM AND WORLD
EXCLUDING NORTH AMERICA

plays@samuelfrench.co.uk

020 7255 4302/01

Each title is subject to availability from Samuel French, depending upon country of performance.

CAUTION: Professional and amateur producers are hereby warned that SERIOUS CHARGE is subject to a licensing fee. Publication of this play does not imply availability for performance. Both amateurs and professionals considering a production are strongly advised to apply to the appropriate agent before starting rehearsals, advertising, or booking a theatre. A licensing fee must be paid whether the title is presented for charity or gain and whether or not admission is charged.

The professional rights in this play are controlled by Eric Glass Ltd, 25 Ladbroke Crescent, London W11 1PS.

No one shall make any changes in this title for the purpose of production. No part of this book may be reproduced, stored in a retrieval system, or transmitted in any form, by any means, now known or yet to be invented, including mechanical, electronic, photocopying, recording, videotaping, or otherwise, without the prior written permission of the publisher. No one shall upload this title, or part of this title, to any social media websites.

The right of Philip King to be identified as author of this work has been asserted in accordance with Section 77 of the Copyright, Designs and Patents Act 1988.

SERIOUS CHARGE

Presented by H. J. Barlow at the Garrick Theatre, London, on the 17th February 1955, with the following cast of characters:

(in the order of their appearance)

MRS PHILLIPS, Howard's mother	Olga Lindo
HESTER BYFIELD	Victoria Hopper
EVA BROWNING, the maid	Valerie Gaunt
HOWARD PHILLIPS	Patrick McGoohan
LARRY THOMPSON	Anthony Wager
MARY WILLIAMS	Barbara Atkinson
MR GRANGER	Frank Lawton
JOHNSON	John Jarvis
ROBERTS	Aubrey Richins

The play directed by MARTIN LANDAU

Settings designed by RONALD BROWN

SYNOPSIS OF SCENES

ACT I
SCENE 1 A room in the Vicarage, Bellington. Late November. 9 p.m.
SCENE 2 The same. A fortnight later. 9.30 p.m.

ACT II
SCENE 1 The same. Two days later. 8 p.m.
SCENE 2 The same. Three days later. 5.30 p.m.

ACT III
The living-room in Hester Byfield's cottage. Three days later. 9.30 p.m.

Time—the present

To face page 1—Serious Charge

Photograph by Layland-Ross

SERIOUS CHARGE

ACT I

Scene 1

SCENE—*A room in the Vicarage, Bellington. Late November. 9 p.m.*
It is a comfortable, light room and the furnishings, though not expensive, are all in beautiful taste. There is only one door, C of the back wall, giving access to the hall, with the front door off L, and other parts of the house off R. There is a deep bay window L and the fireplace is R. A sofa stands RC with a table behind it for drinks, there is an easy chair LC and a flat-topped desk by the window L. In addition, there are, of course, all the usual chairs, tables and dressing. A radiogram stands up R. The telephone is on the desk. At night the room is lit by electric-candle wall-brackets over the fireplace and R and L of the door, and with a table-lamp on the desk and a standard lamp above the fireplace.
(*See the Ground Plan and Photograph of the Scene*)

When the CURTAIN *rises, the room is empty. The window curtains are closed and the wall-brackets are lit. After a moment or two,* MRS PHILLIPS *enters. She is followed on by* MISS HESTER BYFIELD. MRS PHILLIPS *is a pleasant, intelligent woman of fifty-three.* HESTER *is aged thirty; restless and dowdy; a woman who might so easily become an eccentric spinster in later years.*

MRS PHILLIPS (*as she enters*) Come in here, Miss Byfield. (*She moves behind the easy chair LC and straightens the cushion*)
HESTER (*shaking a finger at Mrs Phillips; waggishly*) A-ha! (*She crosses to the fireplace*)
MRS PHILLIPS (*correcting herself*) I'm sorry—Hester. Eva will bring the coffee in a moment. Do sit down, won't you?
HESTER (*twittering somewhat*) Thank you. I *do* love this room. So different from Mr Peters' time. You've made it so cosy, and yet so—artistic—if you know what I mean. What you might call a real woman's room.
MRS PHILLIPS (*laughing*) Oh dear! (*She moves to the desk, switches on the table-lamp, then crosses and switches on the standard lamp*)
HESTER. Why—what . . .?
MRS PHILLIPS. You mustn't let my son hear you say that. You see the décor is his entirely. (*She moves above the left end of the sofa*)
HESTER (*abashed*) Oh—oh! (*Brightly*) Oh, but how clever of the Vicar to get away from the usual stuffy browns and dark greens one finds in so many bachelors' rooms. (*Quickly, and with a rather irritating giggle*) Not that I am in the habit of visiting bachelors' rooms, if you know what I mean.

(EVA BROWNING, *the maid, enters. She is a bright little country girl of seventeen. She wears uniform with cap and apron. She carries a silver tray with coffee for two*)

EVA (*as she enters*) May I come in, ma'am?
MRS PHILLIPS. Yes, do, Eva. (*She sits on the sofa at the left end*)
EVA (*crossing to the coffee table below the sofa*) Thank you, ma'am. (*She puts the tray on the table and stands* C) I've kept some coffee back for the Vicar. This might be cold by the time he arrives.
MRS PHILLIPS. Thank you, Eva. That's very thoughtful of you.
EVA. I expect he'll be starved when he does get in—all this rain, and so blowy, too. You don't think he'd rather have some hot soup, do you, ma'am? It wouldn't take a minute.
MRS PHILLIPS (*laughing*) Now, Eva! I've warned you before; you must stop spoiling the Vicar.
EVA (*smiling*) Oh, ma'am.
MRS PHILLIPS (*smiling*) It's perfectly disgraceful, Miss Byfield, the way Eva spoils and mollycoddles Howard. Neglects me completely.

(HESTER *sits* R *of Mrs Phillips on the sofa*)

EVA (*smiling*) Oh, ma'am.
MRS PHILLIPS. And of course, Howard just loves it—wallows in it, in fact.
HESTER (*with a thin smile*) Really! Does the—er—Thompson boy know about this? He might be jealous if he did.

(EVA *looks up quickly*)

MRS PHILLIPS. The Thompson boy? You mean Larry Thompson, the boy who brings our milk from the farm?
HESTER. Oh, perhaps I shouldn't have . . . I'm sorry, Eva, if I'm betraying secrets.
EVA (*after a sharp look at Hester*) If you'll excuse me, ma'am, I must be getting back to the kitchen. (*She moves to the door, stops and turns*) I—I'll put some soup on for the Vicar, just in case.

(EVA *exits hurriedly*)

MRS PHILLIPS. Oh, Miss Byfield—(*quickly*) I'm sorry—Hester, you shouldn't have done that. Poor Eva! You embarrassed her terribly.
HESTER. I'm sorry, but naturally I thought you knew.
MRS PHILLIPS (*pouring the coffee*) Black or white?
HESTER. Oh, white if you don't mind. Didn't you know?
MRS PHILLIPS. What? That Eva and Larry Thompson are—er—"walking out"? No, I didn't know.
HESTER. Well, that is the general impression in the village, I understand. Not that I pay the slightest attention to village gossip, of course. But I have seen them together quite a lot myself.

(MRS PHILLIPS *hands a cup of coffee to Hester and proffers the sugar*)

Thank you. No sugar, thank you. They make a well-matched couple. No sugar, thank you. The boy is exceptionally handsome, and Eva is not without a certain amount of naïve charm.

MRS PHILLIPS. Eva is a very sweet, and, I think, bonny girl. She'll make a wonderful wife one day—for the right man. I'm not sure that Larry—but, good heavens, they're both only children yet.

HESTER. You don't like the boy?

MRS PHILLIPS (*laughing, but definitely chiding*) Now, now! You mustn't pick me up so quickly. I didn't say I didn't *like* him. I don't know him well enough to form a definite opinion.

HESTER. I think it's a pity he is no longer in the choir.

MRS PHILLIPS (*not very interested*) Oh, was he in the choir? I didn't know.

HESTER. In a small community like ours it is almost inevitable that everyone knows everyone else's business—within limits, if you know what I mean.

MRS PHILLIPS. I think I do.

HESTER (*rising; coffee-cup in hand*) As I was saying—(*she moves to the fireplace*) in a large city like London, of course—well, I know for a fact—I have an aunt in Kensington, you know; lives in a flat—and she doesn't even know the people above her, below her, or even across the hall.

MRS PHILLIPS. That has its advantages.

HESTER. Personally I shouldn't like it at all. I like to feel that I am surrounded by friends. And of course, in a small village, it simply does not do to be—what shall I say—well—er—stand-offish.

MRS PHILLIPS (*after a slight pause*) No—no, I suppose not. Of course, Howard and I have only been here in Bellington for four months, and since our arrival I have been fully occupied with getting the Vicarage put in order. I do hope I am not regarded as—er—stand-offish.

HESTER (*gushingly*) Of course not, dear Mrs Phillips, of course not. Everyone knows what a disgraceful state old Mr Peters left the Vicarage in. You must have worked like a black to get it all so charming, and in such a short time, too. (*She wanders behind the sofa to the table* LC *and puts her cup on it*)

MRS PHILLIPS. Howard has been a great help. He really has quite a flair for interior decorations. I never realized it until we came down here.

HESTER (*looking around*) Oh, I can see he has; quite a flair. One would never think it—meeting him. One usually thinks of artistic men as being rather—well, you know what I mean. (*She moves to* L *of the sofa*)

MRS PHILLIPS. No, I'm afraid I . . .

(*The telephone rings*)

(*She rises, crosses to the telephone and lifts the receiver*) Excuse me. (*Into the telephone*) The Vicarage, Bellington . . . Oh, is that you, Howard? . . . Where are you speaking from? I expected you home long ago . . . Oh, I see . . . No, of course you couldn't . . .

(HESTER *wanders to the fireplace and stands facing it*)

Is what? . . . (*She looks towards Hester. With a smile*) I'm afraid so, darling . . . No, certainly not . . . I shall expect you in ten minutes. Good-bye. (*Quickly*) Oh, Howard, Eva is very anxious to hot up some soup for you . . . (*She laughs*) I *did* tell her, but I'm afraid you'll have to face it . . . Bye-bye. (*She replaces the receiver*) That was Howard. (*She crosses to* C) He's—er—sorry he hasn't got home earlier.

HESTER (*crossing above the sofa to* R *of Mrs Phillips*) But the choir practice is over now, surely?

MRS PHILLIPS (*smiling*) Oh yes, but he's gone to see his girl friend.

HESTER (*looking up quickly; sharply*) His girl friend?

MRS PHILLIPS. That's what I call her. Actually she is over seventy, I understand, and a confirmed invalid.

HESTER (*unable to hide a gasp of relief*) Oh! Oh, I see. You were joking.

MRS PHILLIPS. Her name is Mrs White. She lives at . . .

HESTER (*breaking below the sofa to the fireplace*) *Her!* Old Mrs White out at Leven. Oh yes, I know *all* about her. Bed-ridden for years, and always imagines she is about to die. She isn't, of course. She'll go on for years yet.

(MRS PHILLIPS *is about to speak*)

Fancy expecting him to go out there on a night like this. The road to her cottage is in a terrible condition. Don't be surprised if the Vicar isn't ringing again very soon, to tell you that his car is bogged down in all the mud there must be up there.

MRS PHILLIPS. Oh, I hope not. I want him to drive you home. (*She sits on the sofa at the left end*)

HESTER. Oh, that's very kind of you, but I . . .

MRS PHILLIPS (*quickly*) It was very kind of you to come at all on such a bad night.

HESTER. I have so much wanted to get to know you; really know you, I mean, before you begin—er—moving about the parish. You haven't done any visiting yet, I take it. (*She sits* R *of Mrs Phillips on the sofa*)

MRS PHILLIPS. Visiting? Oh, I see what you mean. No, I haven't.

HESTER. But you will be doing, of course?

MRS PHILLIPS. When Howard told me that he had got this living—it's his first, you know—and asked me to come down here and keep house for him, I agreed on the strict understanding that he did not expect me to become the Vicar's help.

HESTER. But, surely . . .

MRS PHILLIPS. I am Howard's mother—not his wife. I am afraid I am not exactly the "ministering angel" type. No. I hope to make friends, of course, but parochial duties—definitely not.

HESTER. But isn't that going to be a little hard on the Vicar?

MRS PHILLIPS. Perhaps it will encourage him to find a wife more quickly.

HESTER (*with a quick look up*) Oh!

MRS PHILLIPS. It is high time he was married. He's thirty. Most vicars I know were married with a vicarage full of screaming, half-starved children at his age.

HESTER. Really, Mrs Phillips, you do say the most extraordinary things.

MRS PHILLIPS. Do I? Is it so extraordinary to want to see my son married and off my hands, as it were? I am not a possessive mother. Once Howard is married—(*with a gesture*) I'm off. (*She rises, moves to the table* LC, *picks up Hester's cup and puts it on the coffee tray*)

HESTER. Er—"off"? Off where?

MRS PHILLIPS. Ever since I was a girl I have wanted to travel, but never had the opportunity. Once Howard is married I shall be perfectly free—free to roam the world.

HESTER. Oh, oh, I see. Travel—yes. Very nice, of course, if one has the money.

MRS PHILLIPS. Money! My dear Hester, I have no money.

HESTER. Then . . .

MRS PHILLIPS. I have a pair of hands and a certain amount of brain. I shall work.

HESTER. Work?

MRS PHILLIPS. Yes—why not? I think I shall become a stewardess on a liner.

HESTER. Good heavens!

MRS PHILLIPS. And the sooner the better. So, Hester, if you know of any eligible female who would take Howard off my hands . . . Are there any in the village?

(*There is a pause*)

HESTER (*furious, but embarrassed*) I—I . . . (*She looks at Mrs Phillips for a moment, then looks away, dives her hand into her bag, extracts her handkerchief and violently rubs her nose with it*)

MRS PHILLIPS (*realizing that she has said quite the wrong thing*) Oh! (*She wants to laugh, but restrains herself*) Er—more coffee—er—Hester?

HESTER (*rising*) No, no thank you. You know I think I should be getting home. The rain sounds as if it is easing a little.

MRS PHILLIPS. But you can't possibly walk home in this. Howard will be here at any moment. You must let him drive you back.

HESTER. No, no. I couldn't dream of troubling him.

MRS PHILLIPS. And I couldn't dream of letting you catch pneumonia. (*She puts Hester down on the sofa*) Sit down at once.

(HESTER *sits on the sofa at the right end*)

I can be very masterful, you know.

(*There is a rather awkward silence*)

(*She crosses to the table down* R; *her hand moves automatically to a cigarette box, she picks it up and takes out a cigarette. Suddenly*) Oh, I'm so sorry, I never thought to ask you—(*she holds out the box to Hester*) do you smoke?

HESTER (*in a very subdued voice*) No. No, I'm afraid I don't.

MRS PHILLIPS (*replacing the box on the table*) You don't like it? (*She lights her cigarette with the table lighter*)

HESTER. It isn't that I don't like it; it's just that I've never tried.

MRS PHILLIPS. Oh, I see. You're very wise. It's an expensive habit. Do you mind if we have the radio on? There's a concert I rather wanted to hear.

HESTER (*very subdued*) I should love it.

(MRS PHILLIPS *moves to the radiogram up* R, *switches it on, then returns to the fireplace*)

MRS PHILLIPS (*making conversation*) Have you a television set at home?

HESTER (*quietly*) No.

(*The strains of Sibelius' "Swan of Tuonela" are heard from the radio*)

MRS PHILLIPS. I tell Howard he has to get one if he wants me to spend the winter down here. He won't, of course, but . . . (*She listens*) Ah, Sibelius! Lovely.

HESTER (*suddenly*) Mrs Phillips.

MRS PHILLIPS (*after a quick look at Hester*) Yes?

HESTER. Do you like me?

MRS PHILLIPS. Why, of course, Hester, I . . .

HESTER. No, please don't just say "of course" like that. (*She pauses*) I like you. I admire you tremendously and I envy you.

MRS PHILLIPS. Envy me?

HESTER. Your outlook on life; your independence and your courage. I suppose you think me a—a . . . How old do you think I am?

MRS PHILLIPS. Oh, Hester, really!
HESTER. Go on, tell me, honestly.
MRS PHILLIPS. I will not. I've always found that when one is asked to guess a person's age one is so terrified of saying the wrong thing one goes to the other extreme and says something quite ridiculous.
HESTER. I'm thirty.
MRS PHILLIPS. Oh. (*She pauses*) The same age as Howard.
HESTER. You thought I was more.
MRS PHILLIPS. I—I hadn't even begun to think about it.
HESTER. But I know you do. Everyone does. I *am* old for my age. You see I've lived in this village all my life. I never had the chance to get away when I was younger. Up to two years ago I was nursing a sick mother; scarcely ever left her side, except for an occasional function in the village hall, and, of course, teaching at the Sunday School. So often when mother had one of her really bad nights and I had to sit by her side, I used to dream of all the things I would do when she—went. Does that sound awful?
MRS PHILLIPS. No, it does not. (*She sits on the fireside stool down* R)
HESTER. Then—when she did—go, and I was completely free, I found I hadn't the courage to do one of the things I'd dreamed about. I just stayed on in the same little house I was born in. I suppose I am lucky, in a way. I have enough to live on.
MRS PHILLIPS. Very lucky indeed. And thirty isn't old, you know.
HESTER (*unhappily*) No—not really.
MRS PHILLIPS. And you have all your friends in the village.
HESTER (*almost puzzled*) My friends?
MRS PHILLIPS. You said, just now, that that was why you liked village life—surrounded by all your friends.
HESTER (*suddenly dissolving into low sobbing*) I haven't—I haven't any . . . (*She buries her face in her hands*)

(MRS PHILLIPS *rises, goes to the radio, switches it off, then moves to* R *of the sofa and perches herself on the arm*)

MRS PHILLIPS. Come along now. (*She gathers Hester to her*) Listen. Perhaps I can help you.
HESTER (*sniffing; almost hysterically*) Will you? May I come and see you—often? I feel if only I could talk to you—you'd understand. You see . . .
MRS PHILLIPS. Not now. Howard will be here any minute. You don't want him to see you've been crying.
HESTER (*rising and moving up* C) No, no. The Vicar mustn't see me like this. Please—please let me go home now. I don't mind the rain—honestly.

(*The sounds of a car arriving and stopping are heard off*)

MRS PHILLIPS (*rising and moving to* R *of Hester*) You're too late. He's here.

HESTER. He mustn't see me like this. I look a fright. Please what can I do?

MRS PHILLIPS (*trying to be patient*) You know where the bathroom is. (*She crosses and opens the door*) Pop up and wash your face.

HESTER (*scurrying to the door*) Oh, thank you. Thank . . .

MRS PHILLIPS. And you'll find some powder in my bedroom. Dab some on your nose. It has quite a cheering effect I find.

HESTER. Powder? But I couldn't. I never have. I wouldn't know how.

(EVA *appears in the doorway from* R)

EVA. Excuse me, ma'am. The Vicar's back. May I take the tray?

HESTER (*quickly*) Excuse me.

(HESTER *darts out of the room to* R. EVA *watches her off in astonishment*)

EVA (*turning to Mrs Phillips*) Can I take the tray?

MRS PHILLIPS (*with her hand to her head*) My dear child, you can take the tray—(*she does not say this snappily, it is merely the reaction from Hester*) you can take the table, you can take the carpet if you like. (*She crosses and sits on the firestool*)

EVA (*staring at her*) Aren't you feeling well, ma'am? (*She moves down* C)

MRS PHILLIPS. I feel like death. I want an aspirin. No, I don't, I want a drink. And by heaven I'll have one. (*She rises, moves to the table above the sofa and pours a drink for herself*)

(EVA *moves to the coffee table.*

HOWARD PHILLIPS *breezes in from* L. *He is aged thirty, is good-looking and there is nothing "parsonic" in his manner. He carries two books and an evening paper*)

HOWARD (*as he enters; cheerfully*) Well, well, well! (*He crosses to the desk*) Here we are.

MRS PHILLIPS (*almost wildly*) Eva, take the carpet—I mean the tray.

HOWARD (*turning*) Eh? Mother, have you been hitting the bottle?

MRS PHILLIPS (*pointing to the door*) Eva.

EVA (*picking up the coffee tray, rather scared*) Yes'm. Just going. (*She moves to the door*) I've got you some nice hot soup, sir.

HOWARD (*wailing*) I don't want any soup. (*He puts the books and paper on the desk*)

MRS PHILLIPS (*almost snapping*) Yes you do. Eva, bring it in.

EVA (*goggling*) Yes'm.

MRS PHILLIPS. And, Eva, flavour it heavily with arsenic.

EVA. Yes'm.

(EVA *darts out to* R, *leaving the door open*)

HOWARD (*picking up his pipe from the desk and prodding it*) Here, I say! What the . . .?

MRS PHILLIPS. You brute!

HOWARD (*blankly*) Eh?

MRS PHILLIPS. You sadistic brute. How could you do such a thing to your poor old mother?

HOWARD. Now what on earth are you . . .? (*He laughs*) Oh, I see. You mean the Byfield.

MRS PHILLIPS (*muttering heavily*) I mean the Byfield.

HOWARD. Oh, you poor darling. Was she heavy going? Anyway, she's gone now.

MRS PHILLIPS (*suddenly realizing the door is open*) Oh my! (*She almost runs to the door, shuts it and stands with her back to it. In a low voice*) She has *not* gone. (*She points to the ceiling*)

HOWARD. Not?

MRS PHILLIPS. Not. She's upstairs.

HOWARD. What's she doing up there? Or shouldn't I ask?

MRS PHILLIPS (*moving to the sofa and sitting*) I sincerely hope she's pulling herself together.

HOWARD (*gaping*) Pulling herself together—don't tell me you've had to cope with tears?

MRS PHILLIPS. Tears, her life story—the lot!

HOWARD. Oh, you poor darling. (*He moves down* C)

MRS PHILLIPS. If you say that again, my son, I'll hit you. And take that smug expression off your face. You're not counting the Easter collection now.

HOWARD (*protesting*) Really, mother, you do say the most extraordinary things. (*He sits on the left arm of the sofa*)

MRS PHILLIPS (*with a wild gesture*) Her words! Her very words!

HOWARD. Hers? Miss Byfield's?

MRS PHILLIPS. Miss Byfield's—Hester's.

HOWARD (*with a look of surprise, then a laugh*) Hester's! I say! That's pretty rapid, isn't it? "Hester", eh?

MRS PHILLIPS. That was just a preliminary to everything else. We were half-way through the fish when she asked me if I wouldn't please call her Hester. I had my mouth full at the time, and was trying to cope with a bone. I nearly choked.

HOWARD. Oh, you poor darling. But what has been going on for heaven's sake? What made her . . .?

MRS PHILLIPS. I can't go into all that now, she'll be back at any moment.

(*There is a knock at the door.* HOWARD *rises and backs down* L)

(*She rises*) Here she is. (*She crosses to the door and opens it*) Come in, Hester, there's no need to knock. (*She opens the door wide*)

(EVA *is revealed on the threshold. She carries a tray with a bowl of soup and the etceteras.* MRS PHILLIPS, *seeing Eva, makes a whinnying noise, accompanied by a broad gesture of despair, and moves down* R)

EVA. It's only me, ma'am. I couldn't manage the door; the tray, you see.

MRS PHILLIPS. Yes, I see.

EVA (*moving to the table* LC) I've brought the Vicar's soup. Have it while it's nice and hot, sir, won't you? You must be awfully cold. (*She puts the tray on the table* LC *and moves to the chair up* L)

HOWARD. My dear Eva, I haven't just returned from—er—Greenland's Icy Mountains.

EVA (*setting the chair above the table* LC) Here we are, sir.

(HESTER *appears in the doorway from* R)

(*She sees Hester. Dejectedly*) Oh.

MRS PHILLIPS (*following Eva's glance*) Oh! Come in—er—Hester. Howard is back, and Eva has just brought in this lovely . . . Ough! (*She turns away in disgust*)

HESTER (*twittering; not too happily*) Oh, I mustn't disturb the Vicar if he's going to . . . Good evening, Vicar.

HOWARD. Good evening, Miss Byfield. Come in. You are not disturbing me in the least. I haven't the slightest intention of having this—(*he points to the soup*) concoction of Eva's.

EVA. Oh, sir, it isn't a concoction, as you call it. It's beautiful soup.

HOWARD. That may be, my child, but I have just had a glass of beer.

EVA. Oh!

HOWARD. Yes. And I never mix my drinks.

EVA (*after a slight pause*) There's a bit of cold chicken . . .

MRS PHILLIPS (*sweetly, with perhaps a suggestion of acid in her voice as well*) Eva. Go to bed.

(HOWARD *picks up the tray and hands it to Eva.* HESTER *stands above the sofa*)

EVA (*moving involuntarily to the door; bewildered*) Bed, ma'am? But it's only nine o'clock.

MRS PHILLIPS. Then go and dance the Can-Can on the village green.

(EVA *exits.* HOWARD *closes the door and brings* HESTER *down* C)

HOWARD. I—I—feel I should apologize for my dear mother, Miss Byfield. You see she is insane, but no doubt you discovered that for yourself this evening.

HESTER (*laughing; embarrassed*) I—I—Vicar, really, you do say . . .

HOWARD (*smiling*) We generally keep her locked in her room

from the first Sunday in Advent until Boxing Day. Do sit down, won't you?

HESTER. No, no thank you, Vicar. I should like to stay very much, but I really ought to be getting home. Such a bad night. I—I—thank you so much, Vicar, for asking me to dine with Mrs Phillips. I do appreciate it. I can't tell you how much I—I . . . (*She might be on the verge of tears again*)

MRS PHILLIPS (*to Howard; sweetly*) Howard, darling, have you put the car in the garage?

HOWARD (*complacently*) Yes, Mother. (*He starts to sit in the easy chair* LC)

MRS PHILLIPS (*sweeter still*) Then will you go and get it out again?

HOWARD (*straightening up; blinking*) I beg your pardon?

HESTER (*at once all fuss*) Oh, no, Mrs Phillips, please. I couldn't possibly—the poor Vicar—he must have had a tiring night. Please, please let me walk. I love walking, and the rain doesn't bother me, truly it doesn't.

MRS PHILLIPS. Nonsense! Howard doesn't mind in the least, do you, dear?

HOWARD. Good heavens, no. How stupid of me not to think of it before.

HESTER (*quite excitedly*) No, Vicar, really. I can't let you. I'd feel dreadful. It's only just down the road and . . .

MRS PHILLIPS. Howard!

HOWARD (*moving to the door*) Yes, dear. And, Miss Byfield, don't be taken in by Mother's apparent kindness of heart. She only wants me to take you so that she can come too.

MRS PHILLIPS (*spinning round*) What?

HOWARD (*opening the door*) You love car rides in the rain—(*he turns in the doorway*) don't you, dear?

(HOWARD *exits quickly to* L)

HESTER. Oh, Mrs Phillips, you don't, do you? Not really?

MRS PHILLIPS. What? Like driving in the rain? (*She moves above the sofa*) Oh yes, I adore it.

HESTER (*moving to* L *of Mrs Phillips*) I'm sure you're only saying that to . . .

MRS PHILLIPS. Not at all.

HESTER. I can't say how grateful I am to you for letting me come up and spend the evening with you.

MRS PHILLIPS (*ushering Hester* C) My dear Hester . . .

HESTER. And you will forgive me for—for behaving as I did, just now? You see . . .

MRS PHILLIPS. There is nothing to forgive. (*Brightly*) Now, did you bring a bag or anything? (*She crosses down* L)

HESTER (*not replying to the question*) I don't understand you. But I want to—if you'll let me. You seem so wonderfully happy;

you and the Vicar. You say dreadful things—that is, they sound dreadful to me because—well, I've never heard anyone else talk like that—I mean—and the way you joke with each other . . .
MRS PHILLIPS. We have our sane moments.
HESTER. And you understand each other so well. Mother and I—we seemed to have so little—nothing in fact in common.
MRS PHILLIPS (*almost at the end of her tether*) Hester, may I give you a word of advice?
HESTER. Oh, yes, please do.
MRS PHILLIPS. I'm afraid you may not like it.
HESTER. I'm sure it will be good advice.
MRS PHILLIPS. Snap out of yourself.
HESTER. Er—what? I don't quite follow.
MRS PHILLIPS. You're being too sorry for yourself. You're constantly telling yourself how drab your life is, and you're doing damn all about it.
HESTER (*rather shocked by the "damn all"*) Mrs Phillips. But how can I . . .?
MRS PHILLIPS. I'll tell you what I would do in your place. (*She sits on the right arm of the easy chair*)
HESTER (*twittering*) Oh, please do.
MRS PHILLIPS. Well—don't for heaven's sake think I'm prying into your private affairs, but you're not exactly hard up, are you?
HESTER. Oh, no, I'm quite comfortably situated really. Mother left me . . .
MRS PHILLIPS. You could afford to take yourself up to London now and again?
HESTER. Oh, yes—but . . .
MRS PHILLIPS. Then this is what I should do, in your place. I'd go up to town, and straight to a good hairdresser, and tell them to get to work on me.
HESTER. But I couldn't, really . . .
MRS PHILLIPS. Then I'd find a dress shop—just a wee bit more expensive than I could afford, and again, I'd tell them to get to work on me. I'd come out of that shop glowing with satisfaction; hail a taxi——

(HOWARD *enters from* L. *He wears his mackintosh and carries a mackintosh cape for Mrs Phillips*)

—drive to *Claridges* . . .
HOWARD (*as he enters*) We can't. We haven't enough petrol.
MRS PHILLIPS (*rising*) What? What are you talking about?
HOWARD. I don't know. And I'm sure you don't. (*He moves to Mrs Phillips*) Here you are, darling. Here's your cape. Pop it on.
HESTER. I feel dreadful about this, I . . . Oh, my mackintosh is in the lobby. (*She collects her handbag*) Excuse me.

(HESTER *darts out to* L)

SCENE 1 — SERIOUS CHARGE

MRS PHILLIPS. You fiend! I am *not* coming with you. (*She moves down* L)
HOWARD (*following Mrs Phillips and putting the cape over her shoulders*) Yes, you are. You're not leaving me alone on a dark night with Hester Byfield.
MRS PHILLIPS. Shut up, you fool, she'll hear you.
HOWARD. Have you got your gloves?
MRS PHILLIPS. What do you care whether . . .
HOWARD. And your hot-water bottle and your ear trumpet?
MRS PHILLIPS. I'll never forgive you for this—but never. (*She moves up* C)

(HESTER *appears in the doorway, wearing a mackintosh and carrying a drab sou'wester and her bag*)

(*She sees Hester*) Oh! Ready, Hester?
HESTER. Yes, thank you. But I feel very guilty.
MRS PHILLIPS. Rubbish! Howard, take Hester to the car. I'll follow you.
HESTER. Oh, my bag! Oh, I've got it.

(HESTER *exits to* L. HOWARD *moves to the door.* MRS PHILLIPS, *thinking Howard has gone, removes her cape*)

HOWARD (*stopping and turning in the doorway*) No dodging! you're not out in two minutes, I'll come and fetch you.

(HOWARD *exits to* L)

MRS PHILLIPS (*putting on her cape*) Coward. I must tell Eva we're going out. The poor girl will wonder where on earth . . .

(MRS PHILLIPS *exits to* L)

(*Off; calling*) Eva.
EVA (*off*) Yes, ma'am?
MRS PHILLIPS (*off*) We're just driving Miss Byfield home. We shan't be long.
EVA (*off*) Right, ma'am.
MRS PHILLIPS (*off*) Oh, you might look to the fire, will you?
EVA (*off*) Yes, ma'am. And I'll put the lights out, too.
MRS PHILLIPS (*off; in the distance*) Thank you, Eva.

(EVA *enters from* R. *The sounds of a car departing are heard.* EVA *switches off the standard lamp, moves to the fireplace, sees that it is tidy, crosses to the desk and switches off the table-lamp. She tidies the cushions and puts the coffee table behind the sofa.*

LARRY THOMPSON, *unseen by Eva, appears in the doorway from* R. *He is a very good-looking boy of sixteen to seventeen, with fair hair. He is not tall, but well built. He is very much the "wide boy", inferior to no-one. He wears old flannel trousers, an open-necked khaki shirt, a muffler, a bright but dirty jerkin and farm boots*)

LARRY (*stepping just inside the door; quietly*) Hallo!

(EVA *turns with a scream*)

It's all right. It's only me.

EVA (*moving to* R *of the doorway*) Larry! Whatever are you . . .? You frightened the life out of me. What are you doing here?

LARRY. Come to see you.

EVA. Larry Thompson, you must be mad. Walking into the Vicarage without so much as "by your leave".

LARRY. It's all right. They've gone out, haven't they?

EVA. Yes, but . . .

LARRY. I saw 'em go. (*He leans on the left doorpost*) Barmy Byfield was with 'em.

EVA. Larry, you shouldn't call people names.

LARRY. I rang the back-door bell, but you didn't answer so I thought I'd come in and find you, like.

EVA. Well, you'd no business to. They've only gone to take Miss Byfield home. They'll be back in ten minutes.

LARRY (*with a low chuckle*) A lot can happen in ten minutes. (*He pauses briefly*) Come here.

EVA (*backing away slightly*) No. Larry, please go. If the Vicar found you here . . .

LARRY (*with great contempt*) Huh—him! I'd soon tell him where he gets off.

EVA. Larry, you shouldn't talk like that.

LARRY (*after a brief pause*) Come here.

(EVA *pauses for a moment, then moves towards him and stands by the opposite doorpost, facing him*)

(*He takes her hand*) What's up? Don't you like me any more?

EVA. Of course I do.

LARRY. Honest?

EVA. Honest.

LARRY. Well, what's up? You were supposed to see me last night. Why didn't you?

EVA. Oh, I don't know.

LARRY. Has *he* been saying things to you about me?

EVA. Who?

LARRY. Vicar.

EVA. No, of course he hasn't. Why should he?

LARRY. Oh, forget it. Why didn't you see me then?

EVA. Well—(*she looks up at him*) I didn't like the way you behaved when we were out last week.

LARRY. I'm sorry, I shouldn't have. But we're not kids.

EVA. No. (*Quietly*) And we're not married, either.

LARRY (*after a pause*) Where *did* you go last night?

EVA. I met Mary Williams and we . . .

LARRY (*very sharply*) What did you meet her for?

Eva. Well, why shouldn't I? I met her by accident. She seemed a bit lonely, so I took her home with me.
Larry. And there was I imagining all sorts of things.
Eva. Silly.
Larry. Well when you're in love with somebody . . .
Eva. Larry . . .
Larry. You know I'm in love with you, don't you?

(Eva *nods*)

Well, what about tomorrow night then? Shall I see you?
Eva. Yes. That is if . . .
Larry. There's going to be no "ifs". (*Softly*) You want to see me, don't you? (*He moves towards her and leans over her*)
Eva (*quietly*) You know I do. So long as you . . .
Larry (*putting his arms on her shoulders*) Well then? (*He presses her against the doorpost with his body*) 'Appy?

Larry *kisses Eva as—*

the Curtain *falls*

Scene 2

Scene—*The same. A fortnight later. 9.30 p.m.*

When the Curtain *rises,* Howard *is seated at the desk, writing.* Mrs Phillips *is seated in the easy chair, knitting. For a few moments there is silence, then* Howard *looks up, watches Mrs Phillips for a while, grins to himself, then resumes work.*

Mrs Phillips (*suddenly*) Blast!
Howard (*looking up*) Tut, tut, tut! Madame, if you have no respect for my cloth . . .
Mrs Phillips. I've dropped a stitch.
Howard. That is no excuse for foul language.
Mrs Phillips. What should I do? Fall on my knees and ask the Lord to pick it up for me?
Howard (*laughing*) Mother, you're hopeless. And I was looking at you just now and thinking what a charming picture of serenity you looked. Like . . .
Mrs Phillips. I know—Whistler's Grandmother.
Howard. "Mother", you ignoramus, not "Grandmother". Be quiet. Get on with your sewing.

(Mrs Phillips *looks up*)

I'm busy.
Mrs Phillips. What at?
Howard. As a matter of fact I'm writing to the Bishop.

Mrs Phillips. Asking for a rise already?
Howard. No—you heretic. I'm asking permission to have you burnt at the stake.
Mrs Phillips. Give him my love.
Howard (*blankly*) What—the Bishop? But you don't know him.
Mrs Phillips. No reason why you shouldn't just say, "Mum sends her love".
Howard (*after a pause*) By the way, darling, there's a Jumble Sale in the village next week.
Mrs Phillips. Is there? How nice. What is that?
Howard. Now don't be difficult. You know perfectly well what it is. And you're going to be asked to run one of the stalls.
Mrs Phillips. Am I? And *who* is going to ask me?
Howard. Miss Byfield, of course. She is on the committee, and, I understand, now claims you as one of her dearest friends.
Mrs Phillips. Oh, she does, does she?
Howard. She has told the committee to leave it to her and she will guarantee having you behind one of the stalls.
Mrs Phillips (*serenely*) Oh, yes?
Howard. Oh, yes. And of course, you won't let her down, will you? You will do it?
Mrs Phillips. I'll see her in hell first.
Howard. Mother!
Mrs Phillips. Howard, I warn you. If you do not make it perfectly clear to all concerned that your heretic of a mother is *not* going to get herself mixed up with parochial jamborees, then I shall give you a fortnight's notice and quit. Heavens! I'd rather go and live with your Aunt Lillian.
Howard (*sighing good-naturedly*) All right. Have it your own way, darling, but you *are* getting yourself talked about in the village.
Mrs Phillips. What? But I am never in the village.
Howard. Precisely. That's why. People are asking why you haven't been seen in church since my Induction.
Mrs Phillips. Then you can tell them. The reason is obvious. I have no intention of sitting in church and hearing my own son call me a miserable sinner.

(Eva *enters. She wears outdoor clothes*)

Eva. Excuse me, ma'am. (*She moves to* R *of Mrs Phillips*)
Mrs Phillips. Yes, Eva?
Eva. I'm going out now, ma'am.
Howard (*waving a paw at her*) Bye-bye.

(Eva *giggles*)

Mrs Phillips. That's all right, Eva. Is the back door locked?
Eva. Yes, ma'am.

HOWARD. And the cat in the oven?
EVA (*giggling*) Oh, sir. (*She moves above the desk*) Any letters to post, sir?
HOWARD. No, thank you, Eva. Not at the moment. You're looking particularly gay tonight. Where are you going?
MRS PHILLIPS. Don't tell him, Eva. He's only curious.
HOWARD. Of course I'm curious.
EVA (*giggling*) Well, sir . . .
MRS PHILLIPS. Don't be late back, Eva.
HOWARD. If she's not in by ten I shall go and find her.
EVA (*laughing*) Oh, sir. (*She moves to the door*) Good night, ma'am. Good night, sir.

(EVA *exits, still giggling*)

MRS PHILLIPS. I don't know why it should be, but that girl can converse very intelligently with me, yet the moment she finds herself in your presence she is reduced to giggles and an occasional "Oh, sir". It's unbelievable, of course, but she adores you.
HOWARD. Of course she does. And so do you. I can understand it, of course.
MRS PHILLIPS. Howard! Has Eva got a boy friend?
HOWARD. Several, I should imagine. She's attractive enough.
MRS PHILLIPS. Hester Byfield was saying the first night she came here, that . . .
HOWARD. I thought you didn't listen to village gossip.
MRS PHILLIPS. I don't, but naturally I'm interested where Eva is concerned.
HOWARD. Well, what did Hester say?
MRS PHILLIPS. That Eva is going out with the boy who brings our milk from the farm—Larry Thompson.
HOWARD (*alert*) What?
MRS PHILLIPS. Of course it may only be . . .
HOWARD (*rising and crossing to* C; *very troubled*) Mother, she isn't, is she?
MRS PHILLIPS (*taken aback by Howard's seriousness*) What? I don't know. As I said, it's only what Hester . . . Howard, what is it? You seem very agitated.
HOWARD. It—it isn't serious, is it? Between Eva and young Thompson, I mean.
MRS PHILLIPS. For heaven's sake! Don't I keep telling you I know nothing whatever about it, except that Hester says she has seen them out together. Of course the boy is very good-looking.

(HOWARD *crosses to the fireplace, fills and lights his pipe*)

HOWARD. He's far too good-looking. And he knows it.
MRS PHILLIPS. What—that he's far too good-looking?
HOWARD (*with a very slight note of irritation*) No, of course not. Don't be stupid, darling.

Mrs Phillips (*after a look at Howard*) Oh! I'm sorry.

Howard (*crossing to Mrs Phillips and putting his arm around her shoulders*) Sorry, darling, didn't mean to snap. (*He lightly kisses her head*)

Mrs Phillips. I forgive you.

(Howard *moves* c)

But, Howard, are you worried about this Larry boy and Eva?

Howard. If I knew there was anything in it I should be.

Mrs Phillips. But the boy's all right, isn't he? I mean you don't know any—what is the phrase—"cause or just impediment . . ."?

Howard. I'm afraid I do.

Mrs Phillips. Oh! May one ask what?

Howard. No, darling. That is, I'd rather you didn't. It's the parson speaking now; not your curly-headed son. (*He sits on the left arm of the sofa*)

Mrs Phillips (*with a little laugh*) Oh, dear! "Should a doctor tell?" Eh?

Howard. Yes, in a way. It's just something that, as a parson, I should like to keep to myself.

Mrs Phillips. If it's something detrimental—I suppose you should. I certainly don't want to know, but what about Eva? Will you tell her?

Howard (*rising and moving to the fireplace*) No. That is—well, no.

Mrs Phillips. After all, if she's in love with the boy or likely to be . . .

Howard. Listen, darling. (*He crosses to* c) Let's forget all about it for the moment. After all, we don't know for certain that Eva is going out with him, nor how fond she is of him or anything.

Mrs Phillips. I'll have a talk with her tomorrow; you know—tactfully—see if I can . . .

Howard. Pump her. I know. (*He laughs*) You're a wicked old witch.

(*The telephone rings*)

(*He crosses to the telephone and lifts the receiver*) I'll answer it. (*Into the telephone*) The Vicarage . . . (*He gives a look of despair at Mrs Phillips*) Oh, Miss Byfield . . . Did you want to speak to Mother? . . .

Mrs Phillips (*in a hoarse whisper*) I'm in bed.

Howard (*into the telephone*) Come round? . . . Now? . . . Why? . . . Oh, yes, do . . . We shall be delighted . . .

Mrs Phillips. May God forgive you.

Howard. Where are you? . . . Oh, the Institute . . . Not at all . . . Come round right away . . . Good-bye. (*He replaces the receiver*) She's coming round.

MRS PHILLIPS (*with mock surprise*) You don't say!
HOWARD. You certainly seem to have made a hit with her.
MRS PHILLIPS. I have? What about yourself?

(HOWARD *kneels on the floor* L *of Mrs Phillips and winds the ball of wool which has fallen to the floor*)

HOWARD. Eh?
MRS PHILLIPS. Have you noticed anything different about Hester lately?
HOWARD. Different? No, I can't say that I have.
MRS PHILLIPS. Not in her appearance?
HOWARD. Good Lord, you don't expect me to notice if she's got a new hat on, do you?
MRS PHILLIPS. I think Hester would like you to.
HOWARD. What?
MRS PHILLIPS. She's after you, my lad.
HOWARD (*irritably*) Oh, mother, for heaven's sake!
MRS PHILLIPS. I'm telling you quite seriously, that Hester Byfield is in love with you.
HOWARD. Has she told you so?
MRS PHILLIPS. Not in so many words, but she certainly has thrown out some pretty broad hints during this last fortnight.
HOWARD. But it's—it's quite ridiculous.
MRS PHILLIPS. I think it's rather sad. Poor Hester, she's thirty, and she's sex-starved.
HOWARD. Mother! (*He rises and crosses to* C)
MRS PHILLIPS. Darling, why say "Mother" like that. You know the facts of life as well as I do, and if you don't then for heaven's sake take that collar off and get out and about and learn them.
HOWARD (*crossing to the fireplace*) Don't talk nonsense!
MRS PHILLIPS. Of course, she's highly respectable. She could never think of any man loosely. No, for Hester, it must be the banns; the orange blossom; the lot.
HOWARD. But—but why me?
MRS PHILLIPS. Don't be stupid, darling. "Why me?" Why not you? It would be the perfect match—from her point of view. And, of course, she would make an ideal vicar's wife.
HOWARD. Not mine, she won't.
MRS PHILLIPS. Howard, if it should have to come to telling her that, be very careful how you do it. Hester—the woman scorned! Not a very pretty picture, I'm afraid.

(*The front-door bell rings off*)

Here she is. Will you let her in or shall I? (*She rolls her knitting, puts it in the bag on the table* LC, *then rises and moves to the door*)
HOWARD. You do it, please. Mother, listen. I'll make some excuse to go out. I know! I'll go and see old Mrs White. I—er—said I would.

MRS PHILLIPS (*quickly*) Now don't be foolish. How can you go? Haven't you just told her on the phone that you'll be delighted to see her?
HOWARD. Yes, but . . .
MRS PHILLIPS. Shall I leave you alone with her? (*She opens the door*)
HOWARD. Don't you dare.

(*The front-door bell rings off*)

MRS PHILLIPS. Eager, isn't she?

(MRS PHILLIPS *exits to* L)

HESTER (*off*) You're quite sure I'm not intruding?
MRS PHILLIPS (*off*) Quite, quite sure.

(HOWARD *groans.*
HESTER *enters.* MRS PHILLIPS *follows her on.* HESTER *is now much smarter in appearance. By no means a mannequin, but her hair is neater and she wears somewhat smarter clothes. She carries a new handbag*)

HESTER. Good evening, Vicar. (*She moves down* C) I was just asking Mrs Phillips—you're quite sure I'm not intruding.
HOWARD. No, no. (*He moves up* R. *With a hopeful look at Mrs Phillips*) As a matter of fact I was just going . . . (*he catches his mother's eye*) Ahem—to ask you to sit down. Won't you?
HESTER (*sitting in the easy chair* LC) Thank you. I have just come from a meeting at the Institute. Girls' Club, you know.
MRS PHILLIPS. Oh. You belong to the Girls' Club. (*She moves and stands behind the sofa*)
HESTER. I run it.
HOWARD (*moving to the fireplace; hastily*) And very efficiently, I'm told.
HESTER. Oh, thank you, Vicar. Of course I do my best. I took over when Mrs Peters died. That was—oh, five years ago now. Naturally one couldn't expect Mr Peters to run it, could one?
HOWARD. Well, I certainly hope I shan't be asked to.
HESTER (*earnestly*) I'm sure the girls would be delighted if you did, Vicar. (*She giggles a little*)
MRS PHILLIPS (*noticing Howard's discomfort*) Can I get you something to drink, Hester? (*She lifts a bottle*)
HOWARD. Mother!
MRS PHILLIPS (*replacing the bottle; lamely*) Coffee or . . .?
HESTER. No, thank you. Please don't trouble. We have coffee and cakes at the meeting, you know. No, as I was saying, I took over the running of the club simply because there was no-one else to do it, after Mrs Peters died. Of course, when Mr Peters retired I quite expected and was quite prepared to give up my—er—leadership.

HOWARD. Oh, why?
HESTER. Well, naturally I thought—we all thought, that our new Vicar would be—(*with a little giggle*) bringing a wife with him.

(MRS PHILLIPS *sits on the sofa at the left end*)

HOWARD. Ahem! I see.
HESTER. But of course you didn't, did you?
HOWARD. No—I—I—well . . .
MRS PHILLIPS (*smiling*) There's no doubt about that, is there, Howard?
HESTER (*giggling*) I see Mrs Phillips is in one of her naughty moods again tonight. You shouldn't let her tease you, Vicar. (*With somewhat self-conscious naturalness*) Do you mind if I smoke? (*She takes a cigarette case from her bag*)

(MRS PHILLIPS *and* HOWARD *exclaim slightly.* HOWARD *crosses above the sofa to the desk, picks up the cigarette box and moves to* L *of Hester*)

I—I've rather taken to smoking a cigarette around this time in the evening.

(HOWARD *proffers the box to Hester*)

No, please. Have one of mine. (*She holds out the case*)
MRS PHILLIPS (*somewhat staggered*) Hester, what a lovely case! May I see it?

(HOWARD *replaces the cigarette box on the desk*)

HESTER (*rising and moving to* L *of Mrs Phillips*) Of course. I rather liked it when I saw it in the shop window.
MRS PHILLIPS. It's quite new, isn't it?
HESTER. Yes. I—I bought it in London yesterday.
MRS PHILLIPS (*again shaken*) Oh, you—you've been up to London?
HESTER. Yes. (*She tries to speak casually*) I—I had a little shopping to do.
MRS PHILLIPS. Oh!

(HESTER *smiles confidingly at* MRS PHILLIPS *who is somewhat staggered, but smiles back*)

HOWARD. Buying yourself a Christmas present, eh, Miss Byfield?
HESTER. Oh, no, no, Vicar. I shall be going up to town again before Christmas I hope.
HOWARD (*exchanging glances with Mrs Phillips*) Oh—er—will you?
HESTER (*moving to the easy chair and sitting*) But as a matter of fact I did buy one or two little presents—not Christmas presents,

you understand, but—er—presents, if you know what I mean, and—(*she fishes in her handbag and extracts a small parcel*) I hope you won't be cross with me. (*She rises and moves to* L *of Mrs Phillips*)
MRS PHILLIPS. Hester, you haven't . . .
HESTER (*quickly*) Oh, it's nothing—nothing at all, really. (*She hands the parcel to Mrs Phillips*) Just a little token of my appreciation and—er—gratitude for your friendship and help.
MRS PHILLIPS (*embarrassed*) Hester, I'm very cross with you. You shouldn't have . . .
HOWARD (*brightly*) Don't believe a word she says, Miss Byfield. She's not a bit cross. Can't wait to open the parcel, can you, Mother dear?
MRS PHILLIPS. Er—shall I open it now?
HOWARD. You'll burst with curiosity if you don't.

(MRS PHILLIPS *opens the parcel*)

HESTER (*twittering*) It's nothing, really, you know. Just a little —er—but I hope you'll like it. If you don't I could get it changed.
MRS PHILLIPS. I feel terrible about this. (*She takes a small box from the wrapping and opens it. Quite staggered*) Good heavens! (*She looks at Hester*) Hester! (*She rises*)
HESTER (*somewhat uncomfortably*) Don't you—don't you like it?
MRS PHILLIPS (*very uncomfortable*) Of course I like it, but— Hester, this isn't a *little* present. When I think of what you must have paid for this. Howard, look. This really lovely clip. What am I to do? (*She moves to the fireplace, looks in the mirror and fixes the clip to her dress*)
HOWARD (*somewhat shaken*) Phew! (*With an attempt at light-heartedness to ease the awkwardness*) I suppose I'll have to buy you a new dress to wear it on. (*With mock self-pity*) Of course nobody buys me presents.
HESTER (*moving* c; *not without embarrassment*) Oh! Well, as a matter of fact, Vicar . . . (*She dives in her bag*)
HOWARD (*watching with horror*) Miss Byfield, you haven't . . .?

(HOWARD, *unseen by Hester, looks across at Mrs Phillips and turns his eyes heavenward.* MRS PHILLIPS *almost sniggers*)

HESTER. But why shouldn't I? It gives me so much pleasure. And you *are* my friends, aren't you? I can't tell you what a difference it has made to my life, knowing Mrs Phillips and— and you, Vicar. (*She takes a parcel from her bag and hands it to Howard*) You will accept it, won't you? (*She crosses below Howard to* L *of him*)
HOWARD. Miss Byfield, I really am very cross with you.
MRS PHILLIPS (*laughing maliciously*) Don't believe a word he says, Hester. Can't wait to open it, can you, dear? (*She sits on the sofa at the left end*)
HESTER (*with a little bravado*) Mrs Phillips, I am *not* going to let

you tease the Vicar. (*She lays a hand, perhaps accidentally, on Howard's left arm. Coyly*) I'm going to be on your side, Vicar.

(HOWARD, *not unaware of the hand, opens the parcel and produces a pipe*)

HOWARD. I say! But this is a—a . . . (*He gapes at Hester*) It's a Dunhill.

HESTER (*anxiously*) You mean it's not a good one? They told me in the shop . . .

HOWARD. Good? I've never been able to afford a Dunhill in my life. Miss Byfield, I don't know what to say.

HESTER. Just say you accept it with all my gratitude and good wishes and you will make me very, very happy.

HOWARD (*obviously thinking more of the pipe than of making Hester happy*) Well, I don't know—I . . . (*He puts the pipe in his mouth and draws on it almost with reverence*) A Dunhill!

HESTER (*girlishly clapping her hands*) There! (*She turns to Mrs Phillips*) He's accepted it! And I'm not going to hear another word of protest from you, dear Mrs Phillips.

(HESTER *rushes at Mrs Phillips and clumsily kisses her, much to* MRS PHILLIPS' *embarrassment*)

Oh, I'm—I'm so happy.

(*The front-door bell rings off*)

(*She twitters*) Oh! The front-door bell! Were you expecting someone? Shall I go? I don't want to intrude.

MRS PHILLIPS (*rising*) I certainly am not expecting anyone. What about you, Howard?

HOWARD (*still happy with the pipe*) H'm? Oh, yes, perhaps so— I'll go. (*He moves to the door*) H'm! A Dunhill.

(HOWARD *pops the pipe in his mouth and exits, closing the door behind him.* HESTER *stands looking after him.* MRS PHILLIPS *watches Hester for a few moments*)

MRS PHILLIPS (*presently*) You never had your cigarette, Hester. (*She gets the cigarette box and lighter from the table down* R) Have one of mine.

HESTER (*absently taking a cigarette*) Oh, thank you. He *does* like it, doesn't he?

MRS PHILLIPS (*flicking the lighter and holding it out to Hester*) The pipe? He seems quite ecstatic about it.

(HESTER *gazes at the door*)

Aren't you going to light your cigarette?

HESTER (*starting*) Oh, oh yes! I wasn't thinking. Thank you. (*She lights up awkwardly, with a little cough or two; she tries to look as if she is used to smoking, but fails dismally*)

(Mrs Phillips *replaces the cigarette box and lighter on the table down* R *and picks up the ashtray*)

Mrs Phillips. Do sit down. (*She sits on the sofa at the right end*)

Hester (*looking at Mrs. Phillips*) I do believe you really are a teeny weeny bit cross with me. (*She sits* L *of Mrs Phillips on the sofa*)

Mrs Phillips. I am *very* cross with you.

Hester. Please, you mustn't be. I wanted to do it. You are such dear people. I love you both so much.

(Mrs Phillips *looks up quickly*)

(*Awkwardly*) I mean you are both so kind to me, and . . .

(Howard *enters and stands up* L. *He looks rather grave*)

Howard. I'm afraid you will have to excuse me for a while. Someone *has* called to see me.

Mrs Phillips. Who is it, dear?

Howard. Er—a parishioner.

Hester (*after a slight pause*) Oh! Shall I go? (*She rises and moves* c) I mustn't . . .

Howard. No, no, it's quite all right. I've shown—er—them—into the dining-room.

Mrs Phillips (*rising and moving above the sofa*) Oh, Howard, you can't take them in there. (*She puts the ashtray on the table behind the sofa*) The electric fire has been out for hours. The room will be like an ice-box.

Howard (*moving above the easy chair, hesitantly*) Well . . .

Mrs Phillips. No. You must bring them in here. Hester, you don't mind if we go into the kitchen, do you? (*She moves to the door*) It will be warm in there.

Hester (*twittering*) Of course not, but please don't hesitate to tell me to go, if you would rather I did.

Mrs Phillips (*smiling, but definite*) Now stop fussing. We're going into the kitchen and that's settled. Bring whoever it is in here, Howard.

Howard (*moving to the door and opening it*) Thank you, I will.

(Mrs Phillips *looks at Howard for a moment, then turns to* Hester *who has also been looking at Howard. They are aware of his gravity*)

Mrs Phillips. Come along, Hester.

Hester (*moving up* c) Oh, yes. Yes, of course.

(Hester *and* Mrs Phillips *exit to* R. Howard *stands with the door open. After a moment a door slams off.*

Howard *exits to* R, *re-enters almost immediately and stands just inside the doorway*)

HOWARD (*quietly*) Come in, Mary.

(MARY WILLIAMS *enters from* R. *She is a pretty girl aged about seventeen; of pleasant disposition, but at the moment wretchedly unhappy and nervous. She wears outdoor clothes. She stands just inside the doorway*)

(*Encouragingly*) Come in. It's all right. There's no-one here.

MARY (*moving down* C; *in almost a whisper*) Thank you, Vicar.

HOWARD (*closing the door*) Sit down by the fire. It's wretchedly cold out. You look quite frozen.

MARY (*sitting on the sofa at the right end*) I—I've been standing out in your drive a long time.

HOWARD (*moving down* C) What? My dear girl, why did you do that?

MARY. I couldn't pluck up the courage to . . . (*She suddenly breaks down completely, and burying her face sobs heartbrokenly but quietly*)

HOWARD (*moving towards her; quietly*) Mary . . . (*He stops, deciding it's better that she should have her cry out, moves to the fireplace and stands with his back to her*)

(MARY *continues to sob for a while, then gradually pulls herself together*)

MARY (*presently*) I'm sorry, sir. I couldn't help it.

HOWARD. That's all right, my dear. A good cry does help, doesn't it? Do you feel you can talk now?

(MARY *nods*)

(*He sits on the fireside stool*) Well . . .

MARY (*after a slight pause; very quietly*) I'm going to have a baby.

HOWARD (*after a pause*) Are you sure?

MARY. Yes, sir.

HOWARD. Have you seen a doctor?

MARY. Yes, sir.

HOWARD. Doctor Richards in the village?

MARY (*shaking her head*) I've been to Bradington. I saw a doctor there. I didn't want anyone in the village to know.

HOWARD. And there's no doubt?

MARY (*in a whisper*) No, sir.

(HOWARD *rises, crosses to* C *and turns to face Mary*)

HOWARD. Do I know—the—the father?

(MARY *nods*)

Someone in the village?

(MARY *nods*)

(*Quietly*) Who is it, Mary?

(MARY *is silent*)

You don't want to tell me?

MARY. I—I'd rather see him first.

HOWARD. Doesn't he know about the baby?

MARY. No, sir, not yet. I tried to see him tonight. I haven't seen him for a long time now—not alone, that is. (*She sobs a little*)

HOWARD. I see. Have you told your mother and father?

MARY. No, sir. (*She cries bitterly for a while*) Will you help me, sir? I just don't know what to do.

HOWARD (*moving to her*) Of course I'll help you, Mary. (*He sits L of Mary on the sofa*) What is it you want me to do?

MARY. I'll have to tell them at home. I can't go on keeping it from them. Would you be there with me when I do it, sir?

HOWARD. Of course I will. It's going to be a terrible blow to them, Mary. You're an only child, aren't you?

MARY. Yes, sir. I'm—I'm frightened of what dad will do. And mother—(*she breaks down a little*) it'll kill her, I know it will.

(HOWARD *puts his arm around Mary's shoulders for a moment*)

HOWARD. I'll do what I can to soften the blow for them, Mary. I think your father and mother like me—they'll listen to me, I'm sure.

MARY. Yes, sir. They both think a lot of you. That's why I came to ask you.

HOWARD. I'm very glad you did. (*He rises and moves* C)

MARY. I couldn't have faced dad alone. He's always been quick-tempered. (*With a sudden burst*) I don't know what he'll do. He'll kill Larry . . . (*She pulls up*)

HOWARD (*starting*) Larry! (*He pauses, then crosses to her*) Mary—is it Larry Thompson?

(MARY *is silent*)

Mary, you *must* tell me. Is it Larry Thompson?

MARY (*in a whisper*) Yes, sir. I shouldn't have told you. If Larry knew I'd told you . . . He hates you—says horrible things about you.

HOWARD. My dear girl, never mind what Larry thinks or says about me. It's you we've got to think about. You're not going to try and shield him, are you? The responsibility is his as much as yours.

MARY (*wildly*) I don't know—I don't know. (*She rises and moves to the fireplace*) It's been going over and over in my mind. I don't know what to do. (*Hysterically*) I think it would be better for everybody if I was dead; if I was to kill myself. (*She turns to the mantelpiece and sobs hysterically*)

(HOWARD *crosses quickly to Mary and takes her by the shoulders*)

HOWARD (*sharply*) Mary, Mary, stop it, do you hear? *Mary!* (*He turns her to face him*)

(MARY *quietens down*)

(*Firmly*) You'll stop talking—you'll stop *thinking* like that, do you hear?

MARY. I can't face up to it—I can't.

HOWARD. You can and you will. If you do anything—foolish, if you take your own life you'll be taking another life as well—your own child's. And that, Mary, would be murder. (*He pauses*) You understand that, don't you?

(MARY *nods*)

You'll give me your word—you'll swear to me before God, that you will put all thoughts of death out of your mind. You'll swear that, Mary.

MARY (*in a whisper*) I swear it.

(HOWARD *pats her shoulder then crosses to the desk*)

HOWARD. Now I'll come up to your home tomorrow. When would be the best time?

MARY (*moving* C) In the evening, if you would, sir; when dad is at home.

HOWARD. Very well. (*He consults his desk diary*) I'll be there at seven; is that all right?

MARY. Yes, sir.

HOWARD. Good. (*He moves to* L *of her*) And in the meantime, Mary, don't attempt to see Larry Thompson at all.

MARY. But I must see him—I've got to tell him.

HOWARD. He'll be told. But you're in no fit state to see him. Are you—fond of him, Mary?

MARY (*quietly*) Yes, sir.

HOWARD. Do you think he is—in love with you?

MARY (*forlornly, but without tears*) No, sir. I know he isn't. I thought he was, but—he won't want to marry me.

HOWARD (*moving to* L *of the door*) Leave it to me, Mary, I'll have a talk with him.

MARY (*after a pause*) I—I'll be getting back now, sir. (*She moves to* R *of the door*)

HOWARD. It's very dark. I'd better see you home.

MARY. Oh, no, sir. Please—I'll be all right—I've got my torch and it isn't far.

HOWARD. You're sure you . . .? I shall see you at seven tomorrow then, and meantime try not to worry.

MARY. I'll do my best, sir. (*She looks forlornly up at him*)

(*There is a slight pause, then* HOWARD *puts his hand on her head*)

HOWARD (*very, very quietly*) God be with you, Mary. (*He opens the door*)

(MARY *exits to* L. HOWARD *follows her off. The front door is heard to close.*

HOWARD *re-enters, closes the door, crosses to the desk and lifts the telephone receiver.*

MRS PHILLIPS *opens the door and looks cautiously in*)

MRS PHILLIPS. Oh, you *are* alone. I thought I heard the front door.

HOWARD. Yes. Come in, Mother. (*He replaces the receiver and sits at the desk*)

MRS PHILLIPS (*in the doorway*) Were you just going to phone someone? I can go out if...

HOWARD (*rather distrait*) No, no. It can wait.

MRS PHILLIPS. Shall I bring Hester in now?

HOWARD (*after a slight pause*) What?

MRS PHILLIPS (*patiently*) Hester Byfield. She's in the kitchen. Can I bring her in now?

HOWARD (*with an expression and gesture of weary impatience*) Oh! Yes—yes, I suppose you'd better. But, Mother, for heaven's sake try to—to—well, not get *rid* of her exactly, but...

MRS PHILLIPS. I know exactly what you mean. Get rid of her.

(MRS PHILLIPS *exits to* R, *leaving the door open*. HOWARD *consults his diary and makes a note on a pad.*

HESTER *enters from* R)

HESTER (*fussily*) Ah! May I come in? (*She moves to the easy chair* LC) Business over and done with, I hope. (*She puts her bag in the chair*)

HOWARD (*rising and standing above the desk*) Yes, I think so.

HESTER (*consumed with curiosity about the business*) You look worried, Vicar. (*She moves to* R *of him*) I hope it was nothing—er—unpleasant.

HOWARD (*hedging*) Well...

HESTER (*hurriedly*) Oh, please don't think I'm prying. I wouldn't like you to think that. It was just that you looked so troubled.

(HOWARD *does not reply*)

Vicar?

HOWARD (*almost vaguely*) Yes?

HESTER. I'm going to ask a favour.

(HOWARD *looks enquiringly at her*)

I want you to let me help you.

HOWARD (*puzzled*) Help me?

(MRS PHILLIPS *enters, closes the door and stands up* R)

HESTER (*turning to Mrs Phillips*) I was just telling Howa—(*she corrects herself*) the Vicar—that I want him to let me help him.
MRS PHILLIPS. What at?
HESTER. Well, there must be so many things I could do. Parish duties. I don't want you to think I'm interfering—and of course if the Vicar was married I shouldn't dream of suggesting such a thing, but . . .
HOWARD (*to stop the flow*) Quite. It's very kind of you, Miss Byfield. (*Without enthusiasm*) If anything should crop up . . .
HESTER (*rather dampened*) I hope you won't hesitate to call on me.

(*There is a rather awkward pause*)

(*Hesitantly*) Well, I mustn't take up any more of your time. (*She consults her watch. Without conviction*) I had no idea it was so late. But I couldn't wait to bring the—er—little presents.
MRS PHILLIPS. It was very sweet, but very naughty of you, Hester.
HESTER. Oh, but . . .
MRS PHILLIPS (*quickly*) Now, now! We're not going to fight about the presents any more, but if you dare to send me anything more than a tuppenny card at Christmas—I'll never speak to you again.
HESTER (*after a giggle*) What a sweet person you are.

(MRS PHILLIPS, *acutely embarrassed, turns away*)

(*Her spirits reviving*) Well, good night, Vicar. (*She holds out her hand*) And don't forget—if there is any little thing I can do . . .
HOWARD (*taking her hand*) Good night, Miss Byfield, and thank you for . . . (*He holds up the pipe*)
HESTER (*putting her other hand over his for a moment; with a nervous giggle*) Think of me sometimes when you're smoking it. Good night, Mrs. Phillips. Good night, Vicar. Oh! My bag.

(HOWARD *collects Hester's bag from the easy chair and gives it to her. A door bangs loudly off, then feet are heard hurrying across the hall outside.*

EVA *runs on from* L. *She is pale and has obviously had a great shock*)

EVA (*as she runs in; panting*) Mrs Phillips! Mrs Phillips!
MRS PHILLIPS. Eva! What on earth . . .?

(EVA *stands above the sofa*)

HOWARD. What is it, Eva?
EVA. There's been a dreadful accident—just down the road. Mary Williams.

(HOWARD *stands transfixed*)

She's been run over by a motor-car. I think—I'm sure she's dying.

HOWARD (*to Mrs Phillips; almost shouting*) Ring the operator. Tell them to get an ambulance. (*He moves to the door*) Eva, whereabouts is she?

EVA. Just past your gate, sir, towards the village.

HOWARD. And ring up Doctor Richards. Tell him to hurry.

(HOWARD *exits to* L.

HESTER *follows Howard off.* MRS PHILLIPS *crosses to the desk and lifts the receiver*)

EVA. No need to ring the doctor, 'm. Larry's gone for him.

MRS PHILLIPS (*into the telephone*) Operator . . . I'm speaking from the Vicarage at Bellington. Will you ring—get an ambulance out here at once. There's been an accident . . . Near the Vicarage . . . Thank you. (*She replaces the receiver*) Eva, sit down.

(MRS PHILLIPS *puts* EVA *into the easy chair*)

I'll get you something to drink. (*She moves to the table behind the sofa and pours some whisky into a glass*) Did you see the accident?

EVA. Yes'm. It was—awful. I was with Larry—Larry Thompson—about a hundred yards past your gate. It was dark—Mary bumped into us—she gave a scream and flashed her torch on us—she must have lost her head 'cos she gave another scream and ran out into the road. There was a car coming along, and—it went right over her. Oh, ma'am, it was dreadful.

MRS PHILLIPS (*bringing the drink to Eva*) Yes—dreadful. Drink this, my dear, it will do you good. (*She hands the glass to Eva*) Mary Williams. Is she a local girl?

EVA. Yes, ma'am. One of the nicest girls you could ever wish to meet.

CURTAIN

ACT II

Scene 1

Scene—*The same. Two days later. 8 p.m.*

When the Curtain *rises, the lights are on but the room is empty. The telephone is ringing. After a moment,* Howard *enters from* L, *crosses quickly to the desk and lifts the receiver.*

Howard (*into the telephone*) The Vicarage, Bellington... London?... Oh, thank you. (*He sits on the upstage end of the desk. After a pause*) Hullo?... Oh, is that you, Mother?... Have a good journey?... And how *is* Aunt Lillian?... What?... Good heavens! From her wire I should have said she was dying ... H'm... Just an excuse to get you up there... Well, what are you going to do; stay a few days?... No point in rushing back now you *are* there... Of course I can manage... Eva? No, she isn't here... She was very upset after the Inquest this afternoon. I sent her home, but she'll be here first thing in the morning... Yes, it was pretty grim... Oh, Accidental Death, of course... No, I wasn't called. Eva was and the Thompson boy... I'll tell you all about it when you get back... What? ... Food?... Of course I've had some food. I cooked myself a very good meal... I was just washing up when you rang... What?... Talk to Aunt Lillian? But I can't. You know she talks the hind leg off a horse... Oh, hullo, Aunt Lillian... Listen, there go the pips. Good-bye. (*He replaces the receiver, rises, looks at his watch, crosses to the radiogram, and selects a record*)

(*The front-door bell rings off.* Howard *crosses to the door, opens it and reveals* Hester *standing on the threshold*)

(*Quite startled*) Oh! Miss Byfield.

Hester (*twittering as she steps well into the room*) I *did* ring, but I knew Eva was out, and as the front door wasn't locked, I thought I would save you the—er—the trouble, if you know what I mean.

Howard (*not pleased*) I see. What is it you...?

Hester. I tried to catch you after the Inquest this afternoon. I was there. You'd see me there, of course.

Howard. I'm afraid I...

Hester (*moving to the table* LC) No, no, of course you didn't. Your hands were full, weren't they—the poor girl's parents. (*She puts her handbag on the table, removes her gloves and puts them beside the bag*) I felt so sorry for you; having to cope with all that sort of thing. (*She moves down* LC)

HOWARD (*moving down* RC) What sort of thing, Miss Byfield?
HESTER (*quickly*) Oh, I hope I don't sound callous. I am very sorry for the Williamses, very sorry indeed. They have always been good, church-going, decent living people. I can understand the shock it must have been to them, especially when it came out that the girl was pregnant. But really! When Mrs Williams became almost hysterical and you, so very kindly, took her out of the room, well I'm afraid all my sympathy was with you, rather than with her—if you know what I mean.
HOWARD (*crossing to the fireplace; after a slight pause*) What was it you wished to see me about, Miss Byfield?
HESTER (*rather dashed*) Oh! (*With assumed brightness*) Well, I felt I must just pop in and see you and Mrs Phillips. I wasn't able to call yesterday, so I . . .
HOWARD. Mother is not here.
HESTER (*blankly*) Not here?
HOWARD. No. She's in London.
HESTER. Lon—— (*With a certain sharpness*) But she never said she was going to London.
HOWARD. She was called up there unexpectedly this morning.
HESTER. Oh, dear. (*She moves below the sofa*) Not more trouble, I hope?
HOWARD. As it turns out—no. (*He deliberately consults his watch*)
HESTER. But—will she be away for long?
HOWARD (*hesitating*) Er—a day or two, perhaps.
HESTER (*obviously pleased*) Oh. Oh, well . . . (*With a sudden thought*) But what are you doing about . . .? Will Eva be able to look after you all right, do you think?
HOWARD. I'm sure she will, but as a matter of fact I am looking after myself this evening.
HESTER. What?
HOWARD. Poor Eva—she was terribly upset, what with actually seeing the accident the other night, then having to give evidence at the Inquest this afternoon. It was quite obvious that if she had come back here *I* should have had to look after her.
HESTER. So you are alone in the house? (*She moves up* C)
HOWARD. Yes.
HESTER. Oh! But food. What have you done about food? (*She moves below the sofa*) Have you had an evening meal?
HOWARD. I've managed quite well, thank you.
HESTER. But *why* didn't you give me a ring? (*She moves to* L *of him*) I could have come over and cooked you a meal.
HOWARD. Good heavens! There was no need for that. As a matter of fact, I rather enjoy foraging for myself.
HESTER (*her hand going out to his arm*) But I can't bear to think of you just foraging, as you call it. Are you quite sure I can't . . .?
HOWARD. Absolutely sure.

(*There is a pause. It dawns on* HESTER *that she has not been asked to sit down*)

HESTER (*rather coyly*) Well—er—shall I stay and keep you company for a little while?

HOWARD (*consulting his watch*) I'm sorry, Miss Byfield, but I have an appointment. (*He crosses to the desk*)

HESTER (*moving above the easy chair*) Oh, not old Mrs White again? She hasn't . . .?

HOWARD. No, no. But someone is coming here to see me.

HESTER (*flatly*) Oh! (*Hopefully*) Well, couldn't I go into the kitchen and prepare a little supper for you? You could have it after—er—they've—gone. (*She moves above the desk*)

HOWARD (*concealing his irritation with difficulty*) No, no thank you. It's very kind of you but I have had all I need for tonight. And Eva will be here early in the morning. After my—er—visitor has gone I shall try to get an early night. So—if you will forgive me . . .?

HESTER (*flatly*) Oh, of course. (*She makes another determined effort*) But *must* you see this—whoever it is—tonight? I mean it seems such a shame that you should be bothered when you've had such a gruelling day and are so very tired. Couldn't you put them off?

HOWARD (*sitting at the desk; impatiently*) No, no. Please, Miss Byfield; don't worry about me. I'm quite all right.

HESTER (*moving and standing above Howard*) You know—I don't believe you are. (*She puts her hand lightly on his arm*) If I were your wife—(*she smiles*) I should see to it that no-one troubled you for quite a few days. I should insist on it.

HOWARD (*after a slight pause*) Then, as we both appear to have determined wills of our own, it is fortunate that we are—(*he pauses slightly*) neither of us—attracted to each other in that way.

(HOWARD *has said this with a smile, but its meaning is not lost on* HESTER)

(*Quickly*) And now, Miss Byfield; if you will—(*he looks at his watch*) forgive me . . . (*He rises, crosses below the desk to the door and opens it*)

HESTER (*nettled*) Oh yes, of course. I mustn't clash with your —mysterious visitor. (*She moves to the table* LC *and picks up her bag and gloves*) You seem to have quite a succession of them, don't you?

HOWARD (*standing* R *of the open door*) Succession?

HESTER (*archly*) You had one the other night, hadn't you? And now another. (*With just a touch of sharpness as a new thought dawns on her*) Or is it the same one?

(HOWARD *turns and looks her full in the face for quite a long time*)

HOWARD (*presently; very quietly, but with finality*) I'll see you to the door.

(HOWARD *exits to* L, *leaving the door open.*

HESTER, *with a look of fury, moves a step towards the door, stops, thinks for a moment, then slowly puts her bag under the table* LC *and exits hurriedly to* L. *The front door is heard to open and close.*

HOWARD *re-enters, closes the door, crosses to the desk, picks up the Dunhill pipe, looks at it, and with an impatient grunt, opens a drawer and almost hurls the pipe into it. He crosses to the radiogram, puts on a record of* "In Dulce Jubilo", *starts it playing, sits on the sofa, takes his pipe and pouch from his pocket, and fills and lights his pipe. The front-door bell rings off.*

HOWARD *looks up, rises and exits to* L. *After a few moments he re-enters, speaking over his shoulder*)

(*Quietly but sharply*) Come in here. (*He moves to the radiogram and switches it off*)

(LARRY *enters from* L. *He comes in quite at ease, but at the same time, rather puzzled. He stands just inside the door and looks around for a moment*)

LARRY (*chirpily*) Shall I—shut the door? (*He defiantly shuts the door*)
HOWARD (*pointing to the easy chair* LC) Sit down.
LARRY. 'Fraid I can't stay long, Vicar. I've got a date. (*He crosses and sits on the sofa*)
HOWARD (*crossing above the sofa to* C) You may not want to keep it when I've finished with you.
LARRY (*jumping up*) Here, what the . . .?
HOWARD (*crossing to the desk*) Sit down.

(LARRY *gives an exaggerated shrug of the shoulders and resumes his seat. He takes a packet of cigarettes from his pocket and coolly lights one.* HOWARD *leans on the front of the desk and watches Larry*)

LARRY (*after blowing out smoke*) Mind if I smoke?

(HOWARD *looks at Larry in silence*)

(*He tries to hide his discomfort*) What's the big idea, Vicar—asking me up to see you? Thought you'd finished with me when I—er—resigned from the choir.
HOWARD. When I threw you out, you mean.
LARRY. Goin' to ask me to come back in again? Goin' to give the black sheep another chance, eh?
HOWARD. Another chance to what? Fill the minds of the other boys with all the filth and obscenity that's stored in yours? No, Larry, I think not.
LARRY. You've kinder got it in for me, haven't you, Vicar? Don't like me very much, do you?
HOWARD. No, Larry, I'm afraid I don't.
LARRY (*rising*) Then why the hell don't you leave me alone? You've chucked me out of your choir. I'm not good enough to

mix with your other little darlings, all right, all right. You've got rid of me, so why can't you let me alone?

HOWARD. Let you alone so that you can do more damage in the village than you've done already? Oh, no!

LARRY (*resuming his seat; with assumed tolerance*) Listen, Vicar, I'm tired. I've had a hell of a day. I had to waste a couple of hours over that bloomin' Inquest this afternoon, then get back to the farm and finish off all my usual jobs. I didn't get off till half an hour ago: then I have to come up here and be lectured at by you. Have a heart!

HOWARD. You found the Inquest a bit of a strain, eh?

LARRY. Eh?

HOWARD (*smoothly*) Having to stand up and give evidence, I mean.

LARRY (*not quite sure what Howard does mean*) Oh, I dunno. I didn't mind, not really, I wasn't nervous and shaking like a jelly like Eva was, if that's what you mean. Take more than a Coroner and his merry men to scare me.

HOWARD. You think you're a hell of a feller, don't you?

LARRY (*after blowing out some smoke*) P'raps.

HOWARD. Yes. A wide boy who knows all the answers, but not in their right order.

LARRY. Sorry. I don't get that one. Anyway, I gave 'em the right answers this afternoon, didn't I? Or p'raps you wasn't listening when the Coroner complimented me on giving my evidence so well.

HOWARD. Oh, yes. I was listening. And I agree. You did give your evidence remarkably well.

LARRY. H'm! Thanks. I'll soon begin to think p'raps you *do* like me after all.

HOWARD. Even the Devil must be given his due. Yes, Larry, you made quite an impression with your soft voice; your golden hair; your angelic face . . .

LARRY. That's sissy talk. (*After a long curious look at Howard*) Isn't it? Not that I . . . (*He stops, then indicates that he wants to get rid of his cigarette*) Got a . . .? (*He rises and moves towards the desk*)

(HOWARD *takes an ashtray from the desk and holds it out at arm's length*)

(*He looks at Howard for a second then drops the cigarette end into the ashtray*) Ta! (*He returns to the sofa and resumes his seat*)

HOWARD. I don't think you told them quite everything at the Inquest.

LARRY. What do you mean? I told 'em what I saw, an' that's all they wanted to know. What else could I have told 'em?

HOWARD. That you were responsible for the girl's death.

LARRY (*leaping to his feet, his eyes blazing; in a low menacing voice*) Say that again.

HOWARD. I said you could have told them that you were responsible for the girl's death.

(LARRY *looks at Howard for a moment, then moves to the door*)

LARRY (*as he goes*) Good night, parson.

HOWARD (*without moving*) Good night.

LARRY (*stopping and turning at the door*) My solicitor's going to hear what you've just said.

HOWARD. You pathetic little fool.

LARRY (*desperately*) Here. We'll have witnesses to all this. (*He opens the door*) Where's Eva?

HOWARD. Eva's out—as I daresay you already know.

LARRY. Your mother, then. I'm not going to let you get away with . . .

HOWARD. If you want witnesses you'd better fetch them from the village. There's no-one in the house. But I don't somehow think you're all that eager to have witnesses.

LARRY (*after a long pause*) No-one in the house, eh? (*He looks slowly around the room, turns his head towards the hall outside as if listening to the silence, then closes the door and moves slowly below the easy chair*) You've arranged it all—cosy like, haven't you? (*He sits in the easy chair*)

HOWARD. Quite sure you can manage without witnesses?

LARRY (*quietly*) Quite sure. (*He pauses*) I always was one for looking after myself, really.

HOWARD (*moving to* L *of the sofa; after a pause*) Did it come as a shock to you this afternoon when you heard that Mary Williams was pregnant?

LARRY (*after a quick look at Howard*) I wasn't all that interested, but I reckon everybody was a bit surprised.

HOWARD. But not you, sure? (*He turns to face Larry*)

LARRY (*rising*) Out with it. Are you trying to make out that it was me that had been mucking about with her?

HOWARD (*moving to* R *of Larry*) Yes, I am.

LARRY. Why, you . . .

HOWARD (*pushing Larry back into the chair*) Sit down.

LARRY (*fuming*) You'll pay for all this, parson, just see if you don't.

HOWARD. Sit down and listen to me. Mary Williams came to see me on the night she died. She hadn't gone ten minutes before the—the accident happened. She told me that she was going to have a baby.

LARRY. And she tried to make out it was me that . . .?

HOWARD. She did nothing of the kind. She refused to tell me who it was.

LARRY (*blazing*) You mean you're just *guessing* it was me?

HOWARD. Mary was terrified; she became hysterical. Your name slipped out.

LARRY. It's a lie. I never. (*He rises*) Besides, you say she was hysterical when my name slipped out. Well, if she was hysterical she didn't know what she was saying. She'd say any name . . .

HOWARD. But she said yours, and knowing you as I do, I hadn't the slightest hesitation in believing her.

LARRY. It's all lies, I tell you. Besides, what proof have you, eh? You haven't got no proof.

HOWARD. Haven't I? It's written all over your face.

(*There is a long pause.* LARRY *turns away down* L, *then turns and moves above the easy chair*)

LARRY. You didn't say nothin' about this at the Inquest though, did you? You wasn't so blasted cocksure that you dared say anything about it there.

HOWARD (*quietly*) Mary—God rest her soul—is dead. It was the cruellest misfortune that the fact that she was pregnant had to come out at all, but it was unavoidable. (*He moves to* R *of Larry*) You saw what it did to her parents. (*Sharply*) You saw, didn't you?

(LARRY *is silent*)

And how would your mother feel, do you imagine, if she knew the truth about her son? No. I'm keeping silent, but don't you think for one moment it's because I'm afraid to speak, Larry. But I wanted you to know that I knew. (*Slowly and forcefully*) And I wanted you to know that you are responsible for that girl's death just as surely as if you had stuck a knife in her back.

LARRY (*backing to the desk; almost yelling*) That's a lie! It's a bloody lie! (*He moves down* L)

HOWARD. Shut up!

LARRY. I won't shut up. You've accused me of enough tonight —an' if I choose to deny it you can't prove a bloody thing. But when it comes to saying I killed her . . . It was an accident. An' you know it was. They said so at the Inquest. (*He moves above the easy chair*) Are you trying to make out she committed suicide? 'Cos if you are, you're wrong. Ask Eva. She was with me; she saw what happened. We both did. Mary—she bumped into us in the dark; she was frightened an' ran out into the road, an' that car came along . . .

HOWARD. I know all that, and it's correct in every detail except one. Mary wasn't frightened, Larry. It wasn't fright that sent her running out into the road. It was the sight of you—the father of her unborn child—with another girl in your arms.

(*There is a pause.* LARRY *breaks to the desk then turns to Howard*)

LARRY. It was an accident, I tell you.

HOWARD. What does it feel like, Larry, to have a girl's death on your conscience? Oh, so you've got a conscience. There's hope for you yet, boy. (*He crosses to the fireplace and stands with his back to Larry*)

LARRY (*moving* C; *livid*) Have you finished? Got any more to get off your chest? You're enjoying this, aren't you? You've waited for a chance like this. You've hated me ever since you came into the village, haven't you?

HOWARD (*turning to face Larry*) Don't talk nonsense. Have you ever given me cause to like you? Before I had been here two weeks I discovered you were a thief.

(LARRY *is about to speak*)

All right, we won't go into that again. I said I would overlook that; I did, and how did you repay me? By trying to poison the minds of youngsters four and five years younger than yourself. And now this. In God's name, boy, how can you expect me to like you? (*He turns to face the fire*)

(LARRY *crosses slowly to the sofa and puts his knee up on the right end*)

LARRY (*quietly and with meaning*) I'm not asking you to like me. I never have, and—p'raps that's the trouble, really. P'raps that's why you've got it in for me, 'cos I haven't sucked up to you like the others 'ave. But p'raps I'm not so dumb as they are. P'raps I can see a bit further in front of my nose than they can.

HOWARD (*turning*) What do you mean?

LARRY (*moving his knee from the sofa*) Your guess is as good as mine.

HOWARD. Stop talking gibberish and listen to me. You're going to pull yourself together, my lad, or you'll end up in Borstal, and that would probably be the best thing for you. And another thing you're going to do, Larry. You're going to keep away from Eva Browning.

LARRY (*shouting*) You can't make me . . .

HOWARD. Don't stand there shouting the first miserable and hopelessly wrong idea that comes into your head. You know perfectly well that I can make you, and I'm going to. Let me catch you; let me hear of your being with Eva again, and I'll tell Eva every single thing I know about you—everything. All right. You can get out. (*He crosses and sits at the desk*)

(LARRY *watches Howard for a moment, looks slowly towards the door, looks again at Howard, then moves quickly to* R *of the desk*)

(*After a pause. With a grin*) Well, what are you going to do; cosh me?

(LARRY *does not reply*)

(*He rises. Tersely*) Well, what is it? Something you want to say? If so, out with it.

(*The front-door bell rings off*)
There's someone at the door. (*He crosses to the door*) Come along, I'll see you out.
LARRY (*without moving*) Why?
HOWARD (*puzzled*) What?
LARRY. What's the hurry to get rid of me? Frightened of anyone seein' me here; is that it? (*He moves to the easy chair and sits on the left arm*)
HOWARD. What the devil are you talking about?
LARRY. Might look a bit awkward, mightn't it, if somebody was to find a young lad up here in the Vicarage with you alone?
HOWARD (*incredulously*) What? (*He moves down* LC)
LARRY. People might think things, mightn't they? That sort of thing has happened before, you know.
HOWARD (*after staring at Larry for a moment*) You filthy little rat! (*He slaps Larry across the face with the back of his hand*)

(LARRY *falls to the floor.* HOWARD *moves quickly to the door and opens it*)

LARRY (*when he can speak again*) Right, Mr Parson. That settles it. You see. Just you see.
HOWARD. Get out of this house. Get out or I'll . . .
LARRY (*rising and moving up* LC) You'll what? Chuck me out? You just try it, mister, and I'll show you. You was anxious enough to get me up here, weren't you? Well, I'm here, and I'll go when I think fit, and what are you going to do about it, eh? P'raps you'll get the police up 'ere, eh? All right. Get 'em. (*He points to the telephone*) Ask 'em to come up here. Go on, get 'em. I won't run away. An' when they come you can tell 'em what you like. Tell 'em about me an' Mary Williams—everything. I'll deny every bloody word of it. (*He moves to* L *of Howard*) An' then, when you've quite finished I'll 'ave my say. I'll tell 'em my tale. I'll tell 'em why you *really* got me up here when you knew there was nobody else in the house.

(*The front-door bell rings off*)

HOWARD (*livid*) Do you suppose for one moment that anyone would believe such a . . .?
LARRY. Well, we can soon find out, can't we? It'll be your word against mine. Only I'll go one better than you. I'll have a bit of evidence. (*He pulls some books off the bookshelves up* L *then rushes suddenly at the desk and sweeps most of the things from it to the floor*)
HOWARD. You damned lunatic! What are you doing? (*He moves swiftly towards Larry*)

(LARRY *evades Howard, rushes to the mantelpiece, sweeps several ornaments to the floor, overturns the standard lamp, and pulls some books out of the bookshelves up* R *on to the floor*)

LARRY (*crossing quickly to the door; muttering*) I'll show you whether they'll believe me or not. (*He shouts deliberately into the hall*) You filthy swine! So that's your game, is it?

HOWARD (*grabbing Larry by the shoulder and dragging him back into the room*) Shut up! Shut up! You evil-minded, degenerate little beast. (*He struggles with Larry, but manages to close the door*)

LARRY (*yelling*) Take your hands off me. What do you think you're playing at; mauling me about? Getting me up here when there's nobody else in the 'ouse. Let me go! (*He tries to break from Howard*)

HOWARD. You're not sane. You can't be.

LARRY. I'll show you whether I'm sane or not.

(*They struggle to R of the easy chair*)

(*He falls over the right arm of the easy chair and yells*) Leave me alone! Leave me alone!

HOWARD (*struggling with Larry*) Shut up! Damn you, shut up!

(HESTER *enters and stands up* R)

HESTER (*seeing Howard and Larry struggling*) Why—what . . .? Vicar, I . . .

(LARRY *sees Hester and immediately stops struggling.* HOWARD *sees Hester, moves to the front of the desk and leans on it, panting.* LARRY, *after a moment, begins sobbing and runs to* L *of Hester*)

Vicar—Larry, what is it? What has happened?

LARRY (*between his well-acted sobs*) He—he . . . Miss Byfield—I've got to get out of here.

HESTER. But why—what . . .?

LARRY. I—I don't know how to tell you. He tried to—tried to . . .

HOWARD (*almost as if in a trance*) He's lying, Miss Byfield.

LARRY (*sobbing*) I'm not. Take me away from him. Please take me away.

HOWARD. He's lying, Miss Byfield.

(HESTER *looks at Howard for quite a while. Her expression hardens*)

HESTER (*in a low voice*) My bag, Vicar, I left my bag. Do you mind if I . . .? (*She crosses to the table* LC *and picks up her bag, then moves to* L *of Larry*) Perhaps you'd better come with me, Larry.

LARRY (*still sobbing as he allows Hester to lead him out of the room*) He tried to . . .

HOWARD *stands perfectly still as—*

the CURTAIN *falls*

Scene 2

Scene—*The same. Three days later. 5.30 p.m.*

When the Curtain *rises, the lights are lit. The room is tidy, there are one or two fresh ornaments on the mantelpiece and the shade of the standard lamp has obviously been repaired.* Eva *is at the fireplace, attending to the fire. She is obviously unhappy, and every now and then dabs her eyes with her handkerchief. The sound of a car arriving and stopping is heard.* Eva *pulls herself together and exits to* l. *The front door is heard to open.*

Eva (*off*) Good afternoon, ma'am. It's nice to see you back. Let me take your bag.

Mrs Phillips (*off*) Thank you, Eva. Everything been all right while I was away?

(Mrs Phillips *enters from* l. *She wears outdoor clothes.* Eva *follows her on*)

Eva. Er—yes, thank you, ma'am. I have some tea ready. Will you have it now, or will you . . .?

Mrs Phillips. Bless you, Eva. I'm dying for a cup. Bring it in right away, will you?

Eva. Yes, ma'am.

Mrs Phillips (*crossing to the fireplace*) Oh, thank goodness for a good fire.

Eva (*moving down* c) Shall I take your things, ma'am?

Mrs Phillips. What? Oh, yes. Thank you.

(Mrs Phillips *hands her gloves to Eva, who helps her off with her coat.* Mrs Phillips *turns to the mirror over the mantelpiece, and pats her hair. As she does so, she catches sight, through the mirror, of* Eva *dabbing her eyes*)

(*She turns*) Eva, have you been crying? (*She moves to Eva and tilts her chin*)

Eva. No, ma'am.

Mrs Phillips (*looking curiously at her*) I believe you have. Are you going to tell me that you've broken those priceless china cats in the dining-room?

Eva. No, ma'am.

Mrs Phillips. What a pity! I should have been *so* grateful. (*She moves to the fireplace*)

(Eva *tries to smile, but it is a pathetic effort*)

You just bring the tea in. The Vicar won't be a moment. He's putting the car in the garage.

Eva. Very good, ma'am.

(Eva *exits to* r. Mrs Phillips *moves to the door, closes it, then moves to the standard lamp and switches it on. She looks at the shade and examines it where it has been repaired. She then moves to the fireplace and notices the new ornaments on the mantelpiece.*

HOWARD *enters from* R. *He carries a newspaper, and is by no means his old bright self*)

HOWARD (*moving down* C) Ah, here you are. Getting warmer?

MRS PHILLIPS (*sitting on the sofa at the right end*) Yes, much. Is the car damaged?

HOWARD (*uneasily*) What? Oh no, no. Er—just scratched a little of the paint off the mudguard, that's all.

MRS PHILLIPS. But what on earth possessed them to do such a thing?

HOWARD. Oh—these young hooligans. (*He sits in the easy chair*)

MRS PHILLIPS. Young? They didn't look particularly young to me. Certainly old enough to know better than to throw things at cars. If they'd caught the windscreen . . .

HOWARD (*almost rudely*) Oh well, they didn't, so let's stop worrying about it.

(MRS PHILLIPS, *puzzled, looks at Howard*)

(*With an attempt at brightness*) Eva bringing some tea?

MRS PHILLIPS. Right away.

HOWARD. Good. I expect you're ready for some. (*He rises suddenly, crosses to Mrs Phillips and kisses her lightly but affectionately*) I'm glad you're back, Mother.

MRS PHILLIPS (*very pleased, but somewhat surprised*) Thank you, dear.

(HOWARD *moves* C).

Howard, come here.

HOWARD (*turning*) What is it?

MRS PHILLIPS (*looking closely at him*) You're looking a bit peaked. You're quite well, aren't you? I mean you haven't been just not bothering about meals while I've been away?

HOWARD. No, of course not. I'm—I'm a little cold, that's all. I got down to the station far too early. It was cold waiting. I'll be all right when I've had a cup of tea.

(EVA *enters. She carries a tray of tea for two*)

And here it is. Let me take that, Eva. (*He moves to Eva. With assumed cheerfulness*) Mother, I insist that you buy me one of those trolley things for Christmas. Poor Eva will be going bow-legged, carrying this heavy tray about. (*He takes the tray from Eva and smiles at her*)

(EVA *cannot smile at Howard. She merely looks embarrassed. The smile fades from Howard's face.* MRS PHILLIPS *watches all this.* EVA *moves the coffee table from behind the sofa and sets it below the sofa.*

HOWARD *puts the tray on the coffee table, then sits* L *of Mrs Phillips on the sofa*)

EVA (*quietly*) Thank you, sir. Will you ring if you want some more hot water, ma'am?

MRS PHILLIPS (*watching Eva*) Yes, thank you, Eva.

(EVA *exits. There is a silence while* MRS PHILLIPS *arranges the tray to her liking and pours the tea*)

Your tea, darling. (*She hands a cup of tea to Howard*)

HOWARD. Oh, thanks. And how is Aunt Lillian?

MRS PHILLIPS. Disgustingly well, but, as usual, very sorry for herself.

HOWARD. I hope she didn't keep you caged in the flat all the time you were up there?

MRS PHILLIPS. No, no. I saw to that. I managed to get in a matinée, and I had one day doing the shops.

HOWARD. How awful!

MRS PHILLIPS. Not at all. I thoroughly enjoyed myself.

HOWARD. Buy anything exciting?

MRS PHILLIPS. A few Christmas presents, but I felt I just had to get something for Hester Byfield.

HOWARD (*quietly*) Oh!

MRS PHILLIPS. But after accepting that clip the other day, I *had* to do something. More tea?

HOWARD (*rising and moving* C) No, thank you.

MRS PHILLIPS (*surprised*) Not? But you usually have *three* cups.

HOWARD. I—yes, I will have another cup, please.

MRS PHILLIPS (*refilling Howard's cup*) You're not eating anything.

HOWARD. I'm not hungry, darling.

MRS PHILLIPS (*handing him his tea*) Well, that's as good an excuse as any.

HOWARD. H'm?

MRS PHILLIPS (*dismissing the subject with a wave of her hand*) What's been going on in this room during my absence?

HOWARD (*sharply*) What do you mean?

MRS PHILLIPS (*indicating the shade of the standard lamp*) That lamp shade has obviously been patched up, and I see we're sporting some fresh ornaments on the mantelpiece.

HOWARD. Oh! Oh, yes.

MRS PHILLIPS. You and Hester been playing "Chase Me Charlie" round the house?

HOWARD (*putting his cup on the tray*) I . . .

(*The telephone rings.* HOWARD *crosses to the telephone and lifts the receiver*)

(*Into the telephone*) The Vicarage . . . Oh! . . . Granger! . . . Can you what? . . . Of course. Any time you wish . . . (*He passes a hand across his brow*) You name a time . . . Now? . . . We're just having a cup of tea, we shan't be long. Shall I keep some for you? . . . I see . . . Right. In a few minutes then . . . Good-bye. (*He replaces the receiver and turns to Mrs Phillips*) Granger, the schoolmaster; coming up to see me.

Mrs Phillips. And I rather gathered from your not very tactful replies that he doesn't want to see *me*.

Howard (*crossing to* L *of the sofa*) He did ask if he could see me alone, certainly.

Mrs Phillips (*pouring more tea for herself*) And he's coming in a few minutes.

Howard (*crossing to the window*) Yes. (*He draws the curtain aside a little and looks out of the window*)

Mrs Phillips. That means I've got to control my curiosity until he's gone.

(Howard *turns and looks at her*)

Howard, I'm not quite a fool.

Howard. *Now* what are you talking about?

Mrs Phillips. There's a—a tension in this house that was definitely *not* here when I left it a few days ago. Oh, I know you've had to cope with that terrible accident and the Inquest, but that doesn't account for it—not quite.

Howard. Account for what?

Mrs Phillips. The way you're behaving and have behaved ever since you met me at the station. You hardly spoke a word while we were in the car.

Howard. Driving on those icy roads, I should think not. (*He moves above the desk*)

Mrs Phillips. And since we got back you've done nothing but prowl round the room and—and look out of that window as if you were expecting something to explode at any moment.

(Howard *looks at Mrs Phillips, gives a little laugh, then again glances out of the window*)

Howard. "Something to explode."

Mrs Phillips. I know what it is. The Bishop's given you a fortnight's notice.

Howard. Will you stop talking rubbish and finish your tea. Granger will be here soon.

Mrs Phillips. I am not going to hiccough my way through the rest of the evening, just to oblige Mr Granger.

(Eva *enters. She carries a letter on a salver*)

Eva. A letter, sir.

Mrs Phillips. Anything for me, Eva?

Eva. Oh, it isn't the post, ma'am. This was on the mat in the hall. It hasn't been posted.

(HOWARD *crosses to Eva, takes the letter, moves to the desk, opens the letter and reads it*)

MRS PHILLIPS. Eva, I'm going up to unpack in a few minutes. Would you come and help me?

EVA (*moving to* L *of the coffee table*) Yes, ma'am. Have you finished with the tea things?

MRS PHILLIPS (*obstinately*) No, I haven't. It's a conspiracy, that's what it is. A conspiracy to give me indigestion. Go on, take the tray.

EVA. Oh, I can come back for it, ma'am.

MRS PHILLIPS (*with a wave of the hand*) No, I'll suffer.

(EVA *picks up the tray.* MRS PHILLIPS *glances at Howard, and is at once struck by the look on his face. She rises, crosses to the door and holds it open for Eva*)

(*With a change of tone*) I'll be with you in a few minutes.

(EVA *exits*)

(*She crosses to Howard. Very seriously*) Howard, what is it?

HOWARD (*looking up from the letter*) H'm?

MRS PHILLIPS. That letter. Is it bad news? It must be. You look dreadful.

HOWARD (*moving behind the desk and putting the letter in a drawer*) No, no. (*Quickly*) Listen, Mother. I haven't time to talk to you now. Granger will be here any moment. But I must talk to you. Something *has* happened. Something pretty ghastly. I—I—I wish I'd wired you to stay in town a few more days.

MRS PHILLIPS. Don't talk nonsense. If you're in trouble my place is here. What is it? Can't you just give me an idea?

HOWARD (*moving down* L) No. I'd rather tell you the whole story, quietly.

MRS PHILLIPS. But . . . (*After a long pause*) Howard, you haven't done anything . . .? (*She follows him down* L)

HOWARD. No, darling, I haven't. I swear before God I haven't.

MRS PHILLIPS (*putting her hand on his arm*) That wasn't necessary, son.

(*The front-door bell rings off*)

That will be Mr Granger. Let me know as soon as he's gone.

(MRS PHILLIPS *is about to go, but turns, kisses Howard, then exits to* L, *leaving the door open. The front door is heard to open*)

(*Off*) Good evening.

GRANGER (*off*) Good evening, Mrs Phillips.

(*The front door is heard to close*)

MRS PHILLIPS (*off*) Let me take your coat.
GRANGER (*off*) Oh, thank you.
MRS PHILLIPS (*off*) My son's waiting for you in the sitting-room.

(HOWARD *moves to the desk.*
    JAMES GRANGER *enters from* L. *He is a middle-aged man, with greying hair; stocky, and has a round healthy face. He wears well-worn tweeds*)

GRANGER. Ah! Good evening, Vicar. (*He closes the door, looks around the room, then moves down* C)
HOWARD (*moving to* L *of Granger*) Good evening, Mr Granger. (*He shakes hands*) Do sit down.
GRANGER (*with slightly overdone cheerfulness*) Mind if I have a look round first? (*He looks around the room*) I say. You've brightened the old place up a bit, haven't you? Good Lord! I wouldn't have believed it possible. You should have seen this room in old Peters' time. (*He moves behind the sofa, then* R *of it to the fireplace*)
HOWARD. Victorian?
GRANGER. Stone Age! (*He crosses below the sofa to* C) Well, well, well! (*Suddenly*) I say. I hope you don't mind me snooping around.
HOWARD. Good heavens, no.
GRANGER. I'd like my wife to see this. Do her good. Not much imagination when it comes to furnishing a room, and her colour schemes are a nightmare. (*He moves below the sofa*) Your mother's obviously got a flair.
HOWARD. My mother. (*With a little laugh*) Oh! Mother had nothing to do with this. I'm afraid I'm responsible.
GRANGER (*surprised*) What? You mean you did all the—(*he waves his hands*) colour schemes—curtains—everything?
HOWARD. Yes.
GRANGER. Good Lord!
HOWARD. You like it?
GRANGER. What? (*Uneasily*) Oh yes, yes. Most contemporary. But I can't get over you . . . Good Lord!

(*There is a slight pause, then* HOWARD *collects the cigarette box from the desk and offers it to Granger*)

HOWARD. Smoke?
GRANGER. I'd rather smoke the old pipe—(*he takes a pipe from his pocket*) if you don't mind? (*He crosses to* LC)
HOWARD (*moving to the desk*) Of course not. (*He puts the cigarette box on the desk and pushes the tobacco jar forward*) Here! Try some of this.
GRANGER. I'm all right, just for the moment, thanks. I filled up before I left the house. (*He lights his pipe*)

HOWARD (*indicating the easy chair*) Well, sit down, won't you? (*He transfers an ashtray from the desk to the table* LC)
GRANGER. H'm? Oh, thanks. (*He sits in the easy chair*)
(*There is a very definite silence and uneasiness in the room*)
(*After clearing his throat once or twice*) Well, and how are you getting on amongst us all, Vicar? Settling down?
HOWARD (*moving to* R *of the desk*) Yes.
GRANGER. 'Fraid I haven't seen much of you—except at meetings; but you know how it is—by the time I've finished battling with those little devils over at the school, I'm only too thankful —when I *have* a free evening—to be able to put my feet up and rest my battered body and weary mind.
HOWARD. I can appreciate that.
GRANGER. And, of course, you must have been pretty well tied up yourself, eh? (*He waves his hand*) All this, I mean.
HOWARD. Yes.
GRANGER (*after a slight pause*) But you're settling down all right, eh? Getting to know your way about? Beginning to separate the sheep from the goats?
HOWARD (*moving down* LC) Yes, I'm beginning to find out how I stand.
GRANGER (*after a nervous glance at Howard*) Good. Good. Mind you, they're a queer lot in this village, I can tell you. If they like you, well, you're all right. If they *don't*, you might as well pack your traps and get out for all the good you can do.
(HOWARD *crosses in silence to* C)
HOWARD. You've been here quite a time, haven't you?
GRANGER. What? Oh! Oh, yes. They seem to like me well enough. They've stood me for fifteen years, anyhow. (*He pauses slightly*) My predecessor only lasted two years.
HOWARD (*turning to face Granger*) Oh?
GRANGER (*after a slight pause*) Yes. There was a bit of a scandal going around about him, I believe, so he—er—got out. (*Hastily*) Mind you, I don't suppose for a minute there was anything in it—there seldom is—but you know what it's like in these small places. If they can't find mischief, they'll invent it.
HOWARD (*crossing to the fireplace*) H'm.
GRANGER (*with overdone cheeriness*) But you've settled down all right, eh? Good! Good! (*He puffs at his pipe for a moment*) Of course, if you ever did run up against any, er—well—trouble, I might be able to help, you know. (*He looks quizzically at Howard*)
HOWARD (*quietly*) Thank you.
GRANGER. Not at all. Only too pleased. (*Without much conviction*) As I say, they're a funny lot here. You'd be amazed—the things they get into their heads. Er—how do you get on with Hester Byfield?
HOWARD (*turning and looking Granger full in the face*) Why?

GRANGER (*somewhat baffled*) Eh?
HOWARD. Why do you ask?
GRANGER (*quickly and nervously*) Oh! Now, for goodness' sake don't think I'm as bad as the rest of 'em, but I'm just trying to give you an example of the sort of things they say in a little village like this.
HOWARD (*quietly*) What do they say? (*He crosses to* C)
GRANGER. Well, it's silly, I know, but it's the general impression amongst the gossips that—er—(*he looks nervously at Howard*) up to a few days ago, she was—setting her cap at you.
HOWARD. Up to a few days ago. But not now? (*He sits on the left arm of the sofa*)
GRANGER. Er—no. Not now.
HOWARD. And why not now?
GRANGER (*in a rush*) Look, Vicar. (*He pauses*) I don't enjoy beating about the bush. (*He rises and breaks down* L)
HOWARD. That's been obvious ever since you came into the room.
GRANGER. Eh? Oh! I'll come straight to the point—(*he crosses to* C) I've come up here because I thought you ought to know that there's an exceedingly ugly rumour going around the village about you. If it was just the ordinary "he-say" "she-say" petty gossip I wouldn't have brought it to your notice, but it isn't. It's—it's . . .
HOWARD. Go on.
GRANGER. Look, Phillips, there's no need to take offence at this, but I'm going to tell you exactly what the rumour is.
HOWARD. Please do.
GRANGER. That you got young Larry Thompson up here and tried to interfere with him——
HOWARD. And it is a deliberate and malicious lie.
GRANGER. —and that Hester Byfield came into this room and found you struggling with the boy.
HOWARD. That is true certainly.
GRANGER. I see. (*He pauses*) Well, I'm quite sure you'll know how to deal with the situation. (*He crosses to the fireplace*)
HOWARD. That's just the trouble, Granger, I don't.
GRANGER (*turning; surprised*) Eh? I beg your pardon?
HOWARD. I say I don't know how I'm going to deal with it.
GRANGER. But surely you'll . . . (*He breaks off*)
HOWARD. What? Deny it?
GRANGER. Yes, of course.
HOWARD (*moving to the desk*) I *do* deny it, but where does that get me? Is it going to satisfy everybody? (*He looks at Granger*) Would it satisfy you—that is, of course, if you'd believed the rumour in the first place?
GRANGER (*coughing quietly*) H'm! I see your point. (*He makes a great show of examining his pipe which has gone out*)

HOWARD (*quietly*) Match? (*He proffers a box of matches from the desk*)
GRANGER. Eh? Oh—er—no, thanks. (*He puts his pipe in his pocket*) You—er—you say you knew this rumour was going around. How long have you known?
HOWARD. For absolute certain, about twenty minutes.
GRANGER. H'm!
HOWARD. When I was driving my mother back from the station just now, someone threw a lump of turf at the car. It wasn't a child. It was a man. Then a few minutes ago, this was found on the mat in the hall. (*He takes the letter from the desk drawer, crosses and hands the letter to Granger*)

(GRANGER *sits on the sofa and reads the letter*)

GRANGER (*wretchedly*) Oh, my God! (*He looks with distaste at the letter*) Anonymous, eh?
HOWARD (*taking the letter from Granger*) Charming, isn't it? (*He crosses and puts the letter on the desk*)
GRANGER (*after a slight pause*) But—until your car was attacked and you received that letter, you say you did not know about the rumour?
HOWARD. Not for certain, but I sensed it. (*With a little laugh*) These last two days—whenever I've appeared in the village, my —er—faithful parishioners have avoided me like the plague. I began to wonder if I shouldn't ring a bell as I went along and cry out "unclean, unclean". (*He crosses slowly behind the sofa to the fireplace*)
GRANGER (*blustering somewhat*) Oh, no, no. I think you're letting your imagination run away with you. I don't think anyone —er—that is—the majority really think that you . . .
HOWARD. Whether they do or they don't, Granger, they are *avoiding* me. I suppose one can't blame them for it. Naturally, they'd rather hide their embarrassment than show it.
GRANGER. Well, it is a particularly unpleasant bit of scandal.
HOWARD. Exactly. That's why I say you can't really blame them for scuttling away when they see me approaching. It would have been bad enough if they'd heard I'd been helping myself from the Poor Box or the Collection Plate—but this . . . It's hardly a topic for idle conversation. Well—witness your embarrassment—and mine.
GRANGER. Perhaps I could do something if . . . (*He rises and crosses to* LC) Look, Phillips, have you any objection to telling me about it?
HOWARD. Certainly not. But first of all I must tell you something that I hoped not to have to tell anyone. Larry Thompson was responsible for Mary Williams' pregnancy.

(GRANGER *shows no surprise, but looks at Howard for a while*)

GRANGER (*quietly*) Do you know that for a fact?
HOWARD. Mary told me so herself, the night she was killed.
GRANGER. Had she told anyone else?
HOWARD. No.
GRANGER (*after a pause*) H'm! Pity.
HOWARD. Pity? Why?

(GRANGER *crosses and sits on the left arm of the sofa*)

GRANGER (*after an expressive shrug of the shoulders*) Look here, Vicar. Before we go any further I think it only fair to tell you that I have already spoken to young Thompson about this—er—unpleasant business.
HOWARD (*quietly*) You have?
GRANGER. Yes. (*He pauses*) And Hester Byfield.
HOWARD. I see. Well, thank you for telling me. It puts our—conversation in its true perspective, doesn't it?
GRANGER. How do you mean?
HOWARD. You're not here, as you said, just to warn me of what is being said in the village. You're here to find out if there's any truth in it.
GRANGER. Well—yes.
HOWARD. On your own initiative or are you representing the village?
GRANGER (*rising and moving* C; *uncomfortably*) One or two people —parents of boys in your choir have been up to see me. (*Hurriedly*) Don't for heaven's sake think that they really believe the rumour, but naturally they would like to be certain there's nothing in it.
HOWARD (*turning to the fire*) Naturally.
GRANGER. I'm sorry, Phillips, I understand how you must feel.
HOWARD. It's nice of you to say so, Granger, but you don't.
GRANGER. You say that no-one, not even her parents, no-one but you knew that Larry Thompson was responsible for Mary Williams' condition?
HOWARD. No-one. (*He turns to face Granger*) The girl came to ask me to be with her when she told her parents.
GRANGER. And she came to see you on the night she was killed.
HOWARD. Yes. She hadn't gone ten minutes before the accident happened. (*He moves below the sofa*)
GRANGER. Were you alone in the house when she called?
HOWARD. No, my mother and Hester Byfield were here.
GRANGER (*brightly*) Ah! Then they saw her here?
HOWARD (*sitting on the sofa*) No, they didn't.
GRANGER (*after a look at Howard*) Oh!
HOWARD (*after a look at Granger*) The girl was in a terribly distressed state. Out of consideration for her I got them out of the way before I asked her in.

GRANGER. H'm. I see. And she definitely named Larry?
HOWARD. Yes.
GRANGER. H'm. (*He pauses*) There's also something about him being a thief, isn't there? (*He moves up* C)
HOWARD. Yes. (*With a look at Granger*) But I never said anything to you about that.
GRANGER. No. The boy did.
HOWARD. Oh, I see.
GRANGER. Yes. He told me about the Mary Williams business, and the—er—theft.
HOWARD. He admitted both to you?
GRANGER. Oh, no, no, no. (*He moves to* L *of the sofa*) But would you mind telling me about this theft.
HOWARD. Very well. It was one Sunday morning just before the service—I'd been in the parish barely a fortnight—I was putting my desk in order. Larry was changing the hymn boards —I sent him to my vestry with some books I wanted leaving there. A minute or so afterwards I remembered a notice I had to read out that morning. I went along to the vestry and as I got in the doorway I saw Larry putting my wallet into my jacket pocket. When he saw me he mumbled something about the jacket having fallen off the peg—an obvious lie. I looked in my wallet. One pound note was missing. I asked him if he had taken it. He said he hadn't. I asked him to tell the truth—to confess, but he wouldn't—he lied and lied and went on lying. It was only when I bluffed and talked about getting the policeman along that he finally confessed and handed the note back. (*He rises and moves to the fireplace*)
GRANGER. H'm. There were just the two of you in the vestry, naturally.
HOWARD. Yes.
GRANGER (*moving below the sofa*) And you never spoke of this to anyone else?
HOWARD. No. I didn't want to make anything of it.
GRANGER (*sitting on the sofa*) But you sacked him from the choir?
HOWARD. Not then I didn't. (*He sits on the firestool*) I lectured him, naturally, but said I would overlook it. But I kept an eye on him. One Sunday I overheard him pouring absolute filth into the ears of two of the youngest lads in the choir. I sent for him after the service and told him exactly what I thought of him and told him that if he showed his face at the next choir practice I'd pitch him out of the church, neck and crop.
GRANGER (*after a pause; slowly*) Yes, I see. (*He heaves a big sigh*) It's a pity that none of this has come out until now.
HOWARD. It never would have come out if I could have helped it.
GRANGER. Yes, but don't you see, as it is now, it's only your word against the boy's.

HOWARD. You don't think that is sufficient?

GRANGER. When I saw young Thompson he told me that when he was up here the other night and you tried to interfere with him, he said he would tell his parents, and you said that if he did you would tell everyone that he was a thief and that it was he who got Mary Williams into trouble—both of which he emphatically denies.

HOWARD. Well, you've heard his story and you've heard mine. Which do you believe? That's what it boils down to, doesn't it?

GRANGER (*rising and crossing to* LC) Yes. And—I've got to be honest about this, Phillips.

HOWARD. Go on.

GRANGER. I don't know what to believe. (*He looks at Howard, then crosses to* L *of him*) Look! Will you try to see it from my point of view? I've known this boy, Larry Thompson, from the first day he came to my school, and I've known you how long—three months? And not very well at that. I must confess I never found the boy to be any worse than any of the other young devils. He was intelligent; keen on sport; nothing malicious about him that I ever saw. Of course, he's left school two years now. He might have changed . . .

HOWARD (*bitterly*) He must have done.

GRANGER. But the trouble is, Vicar, we've only your word for that, haven't we? You must forgive me for being outspoken like this.

(HOWARD *gives an impatient "never mind about all that" wave of the hand*)

You say the boy's a thief and he seduced poor Mary Williams, but the trouble is you can't produce a single shred of proof, can you?

HOWARD (*rising and turning to the fireplace*) No, I can't. Not now.

GRANGER. And you must admit it might appear rather strange that you kept quiet about all this until after he made his accusation against you.

HOWARD. I've already told you why I said nothing about the Mary Williams business. The girl was dead. If I'd told what I knew it would only have caused bad blood between her family and the boy's. You must know Williams, the girl's father, as well, if not better than I do. He's a hot-tempered man. God knows what he would have done to the boy. We might have had a murder in the village.

GRANGER. Yes, I see that, but . . .

HOWARD (*crossing to the desk*) And as to the theft—I'd been in this parish exactly a fortnight. I was a stranger, practically. Even though I should have been in the right doing so, I don't think I should have created a very good first impression by bringing a charge of petty theft against a young boy. (*He turns to Granger*) Do you?

GRANGER. H'mm!

(*There is a definite pause*)

Why were you struggling with young Thompson when Hester Byfield came into the room?
HOWARD. I was trying to throw him out of the house.
GRANGER. Why?
HOWARD (*moving* C) Because he had just brazenly told me that he would tell the filthy lies he has, in fact, told.
GRANGER. Hester Byfield says she heard the boy calling for help.
HOWARD. Of course she did. He intended that she should. He did it deliberately, just as he half wrecked the room. He'd heard the door bell so he knew there was someone outside and he wanted to get them inside. He wanted, what he called, evidence.
GRANGER. H'm!

(*There is a long pause*)

HOWARD (*quietly*) You don't believe me?
GRANGER. I don't know. I'm sorry, Phillips, but I don't know what to believe.
HOWARD. Well, there it is. There's nothing more I can say.
GRANGER. No. I wish there was.
HOWARD (*moving and standing above the desk*) What will you tell them in the village?
GRANGER. Just what you have told me. (*He moves to the door*)
HOWARD. And you don't think they will believe me either?
GRANGER (*moving behind the easy chair*) Frankly, I don't know. After all, Vicar, it wouldn't be the first time that this sort of thing has happened—if it *has* happened. Not only your profession, of course; mine as well. (*He pauses briefly*) And you're a bachelor— (*his eyes wander round the room*) with an artistic flair . . .
HOWARD. And those three facts—that I am a parson, a bachelor and have what you call an artistic flair—add up to the one big fact that I must be a pervert. Is that it? (*He breaks down* L) Granger, for heaven's sake!
GRANGER (*moving down* LC; *hurriedly*) No, no, but I'm just telling what will be in people's minds.
HOWARD. And what is—and be honest with me, Granger—and what is in *your* mind?
GRANGER. I—I . . .

(MRS PHILLIPS *enters hurriedly. She is very distressed*)

MRS PHILLIPS (*moving down* C) Howard . . .
HOWARD. Mother, I'm sorry, but Mr Granger and I haven't finished our . . .
MRS PHILLIPS. Forgive me, Mr Granger, but this is urgent.

Howard, you must go into the kitchen at once and see Mrs Browning.
HOWARD. Mrs Browning?
MRS PHILLIPS. Eva's mother. She's come to take Eva away—now. She says she won't let the girl spend another night here. She won't tell me why; just insists that Eva packs her things at once.
HOWARD. Well, Granger, it looks as if they've reached a verdict already.
MRS PHILLIPS. Verdict? Howard, what are you talking about? What has happened? You must tell me.
HOWARD. I can't.
MRS PHILLIPS. But, Howard . . .
HOWARD. Not just now.
MRS PHILLIPS (*shrugging her shoulders*) Are you going to see Mrs Browning?
GRANGER (*to Howard; quietly*) I wouldn't, if I were you. Let the girl go. It would be better.

(EVA *runs in to* R *of Mrs Phillips. She is in tears*)

EVA. Please'm, don't let her take me away. I don't want to go. I won't go. I don't believe what they're saying about the Vicar, it's all lies. I know it is. (*To Howard*) Please—please don't let mother take me away.
MRS PHILLIPS. Howard.

(HOWARD *does not reply*)

(*She turns to Eva*) Look, my dear, perhaps you'd better go. In a day or two this may all be straightened out—whatever it is—and then . . .
EVA. I don't want to go. I don't want to go. It's all lies.
GRANGER. Eva, do as Mrs Phillips tells you.
MRS PHILLIPS. Go and pack your things. I'll see you before you leave. (*She leads* EVA *to the door*)

(EVA, *sobbing, exits*)

(*She moves down* C) Mr Granger, please. If Howard won't tell me what has happened, will you?
GRANGER. I'll leave you together, Mrs Phillips. Perhaps he'll tell you when you're alone. (*To Howard*) Good night, Phillips.

(*There is a loud crash of glass, and a large stone comes through the partly opened curtains. There is a piece of paper wrapped round the stone.* MRS PHILLIPS *gives a startled scream*)

What the devil . . .? (*He rushes to the window, draws the curtains aside and peers out into the darkness*)
MRS PHILLIPS. Howard!

(GRANGER *picks up the stone, unwraps the piece of paper and reads what is written on it. He then moves to* R *of the desk.* HOWARD *turns away*)

GRANGER. They've gone. Whoever it was. Vicar, I'm sorry. I . . . (*He breaks off and looks at Howard*) That was a damnable thing to do.

MRS PHILLIPS (*moving to Granger*) What is on that paper? What does it say?

GRANGER. I wouldn't read it, Mrs Phillips.

(MRS PHILLIPS *gives Granger a quick look, takes the paper from him, reads it and gives a quick gasp of horror*)

MRS PHILLIPS (*under her breath*) No! No!

MRS PHILLIPS *sinks into the easy chair as—*

the CURTAIN *falls*

ACT III

SCENE—*The living-room in Hester Byfield's cottage. Three days later. 9.30 p.m.*
It is a small room, Victorian in furnishings, but quite pleasant and very clean. The front door is C *of the back wall, with a window* L *of it. An arch up* R *leads to the kitchen and a door* L, *approached by two steps, leads to Hester's bedroom. The fireplace is* R. *There is a divan* C; *two comfortable wing armchairs by the fireplace, and a bureau with a telephone* L. *The room is lit by brackets over the fireplace, a standard lamp up* L *and a pendant lamp* C.
(*See the Ground Plan and Photograph of the Scene*)

When the CURTAIN *rises,* HESTER *is seated in the armchair above the fireplace, drinking a glass of milk, the remains of her supper which is on a low table beside her chair. She finishes the milk, picks up a box of Christmas cards from the table, then rises, moves to the mantelpiece, picks up a pair of scissors, cuts the string of the box, replaces the scissors and looks idly through the cards. She suddenly starts, as if she heard someone outside. Putting the box on the table, she goes to the window and peeps cautiously through the curtains. She turns, giving a sigh of relief, but is obviously ill at ease. She stands for a moment or two, then after looking towards the telephone, crosses to it and lifts the receiver.*

HESTER (*into the telephone*) Four-two-eight, please . . . (*She waits*) Oh, Mrs Richards? . . . This is Hester Byfield speaking. Is the doctor in? . . . Oh! . . . Well—would you ask him if he would call and see me tomorrow sometime? . . . No, no, it's—it's nothing serious, just that I—I . . . (*She is almost in tears*) If he would call I'd be most grateful . . . Thank you . . . Good-bye. (*She replaces the receiver, dabs at her eyes with a handkerchief, and, making a determined effort to pull herself together, sits at the bureau. She addresses an envelope, then takes a small cash-box from a pigeon-hole, opens it and extracts a small bundle of one-pound notes. She counts out three, then looks through the rest of the notes, seeking a ten-shilling note. Puzzled, she looks in the cash-box, then peers quickly into one or two pigeon-holes. At last, she puts all but the three one-pound notes back into the cash-box and puts the box into a pigeon-hole. She puts the three notes and a bill into the envelope, seals it, lays it on the bureau, closes the lid, then crosses and sits in the armchair above the fireplace*)

(*There is a quiet knock at the front door.* HESTER *gives a little gasp, rises, moves up* C *and switches out the lights. The knocking is repeated, but louder this time.* HESTER *stands in the firelight, breathing agitatedly. The knocking now becomes a hammering. The door-handle is tried, without success.* HESTER *moves to the door, but does not open it*)

(*In suppressed agitation*) Yes, who is it?

To face page 50—Serious Charge

Photograph by Leyland-Ross

LARRY (*off*) It's me.
HESTER (*after a little gasp*) What do you want?
LARRY (*off*) Open the door, Miss Byfield.
HESTER. I—I—no. I can't. I'm just going to bed.
LARRY (*off; firmly*) Open the door.
HESTER. I . . . (*Weakly*) Just a moment. (*She switches on the lights, unbolts the door and opens it a little*) You mustn't keep coming here like this. It's . . .

(LARRY *pushes the door further open, enters and comes past Hester into the room.* HESTER *holds the door open*)

LARRY. But I like coming to see you, Miss Byfield. (*He moves to the fireplace*) And I thought you wouldn't mind.
HESTER. But I do mind, and you mustn't think you can make a habit of it, Larry. In any case it's very late; nearly half-past nine. (*She closes the door and moves down* RC)
LARRY. But I haven't told you the latest—about the Vicar, I mean. (*He warms his hands at the fire*)
HESTER (*sharply*) Larry, I don't want to talk about him.
LARRY (*sweeping on*) Things are moving now and no mistake. They've been chucking more bricks through his window tonight.
HESTER. What? (*Unhappily*) Oh, no!
LARRY. They 'ave, I tell you. And there'll be more to follow. Serve him right. (*He looks at Hester and chuckles quietly*)
HESTER. Why have you come here tonight?
LARRY. Well, I knew you'd be glad to hear about the window smashing. Besides . . .
HESTER (*furious*) What do you mean "glad"? Why should I be glad? You stupid boy.
LARRY (*nettled*) Here, come off it. (*He takes a step towards her*) You're on *my* side, aren't you?
HESTER. I don't know what you're talking about, and will you please go. I—I have a headache.
LARRY (*sitting in the armchair down* R) Five minutes, then I'll be off.
HESTER (*her nerves on edge*) I can't talk to you tonight. I don't want to talk to you.
LARRY (*jumping up; with overdone concern*) Here! You are a bit up-sy-doodlums, aren't you? (*He crosses to Hester and puts his arm around her, preparatory to leading her to her armchair*) Come and sit down.
HESTER (*quickly disengaging herself*) Don't do that. How dare you? You . . . Will you please leave this house? (*She moves* LC)
LARRY (*blandly*) What's up? I was only going to put you in the armchair. I wasn't going to . . . (*He bursts into loud laughter*) Good Lord! You didn't think I was going to . . . (*He laughs*) 'Ave a heart. (*He moves to the armchair down* R *and sits*)

HESTER (*near to panic*) I don't understand you. I don't understand your attitude to me or why you keep coming here. I always thought you were a nice boy.

LARRY. But I am a nice boy, Miss Byfield. That's why I'm here. I'm a nice boy trying to show his gratitude to a kind lady who saved me from being ruined by a nasty man.

HESTER (*moving to the banister; sharply*) Larry, please. I refuse to talk about that. It's too—too horrible. I'm thankful, for your sake, that I was able to intervene, but—(*her voice breaks*) but I wish to God . . . (*She bursts into uncontrollable sobbing and stands by the banister, with her hands over her face*)

(LARRY *watches Hester for a moment, then lights a cigarette and flicks the match into the fireplace*)

(*She pulls herself together. Between sobs*) I'm sorry. It was silly of me to behave like that—in front of you, a young boy, but—I—I'm not feeling very well tonight.

LARRY. That's all right by me, Miss Byfield. Don't you worry; I understand. You've 'ad a bit of a shock, 'aven't you? Rotten when your boy friend turns out to be a . . .

HESTER (*aghast*) Boy . . . ! (*Intensely*) What are you talking about?

LARRY. What? Why, you and the Vicar. You know what I'm talking about.

HESTER (*moving* C) I don't. I don't.

LARRY (*laughing*) Go on, Miss Byfield. You're pulling my leg. Why, everybody in the village knew you were making a match of it.

HESTER. Everybody in the village—knew . . . ?

LARRY. 'Course they did. They ain't blind.

HESTER (*violently*) It isn't true. It isn't true. Oh, how wicked! How could they think such a thing?

LARRY (*waving a hand*) Now, now! Don't go upsetting yourself or you'll be in tears again, an' that would never do, would it? Look! Why not make some more of that nice coffee you give me that first night I come here? It'll do us both good.

HESTER. Listen, Larry. I must try and make you understand. I know you are only a boy, but . . .

LARRY. Oh, will you for God's sake stop telling me I'm only a boy? I'm seventeen. An' I'll bet I know more about life than you do even if you are forty.

HESTER (*as if she has been stung by a lash*) I am not . . . (*She moves up* C *and gives a hopeless shrug of the shoulders*) I do wish you would go.

LARRY (*irritably*) O.K. O.K. I'll go. But we've got to have a little talk first.

HESTER (*moving down* C) What about?

LARRY. Well, things is beginning to hum in the village now, aren't they?

HESTER (*moving to the fireplace*) I don't know what is going on in the village. I haven't been out since—since that night.
LARRY. Well, you can take my word for it that they are. I'd like to bet you there won't be one single kid in the choir next Sunday. In fact, I'd bet you there won't be no service either. (*He laughs*) They're going to hold a meeting of the Church Council tomorrow night.
HESTER. A meeting?
LARRY. Yep. To decide what they're going to do about 'im. An' that's what we've got to talk about.
HESTER (*nervously*) Talk about?
LARRY (*irritably*) Look. Don't keep on . . . Look! Why don't you sit down, Miss Byfield? You're all of a dither. I don't know what you're worrying about. You're not sorry you started all this, are you?
HESTER. What do you mean—I started it?
LARRY. Well, you did, didn't you?
HESTER (*at sea*) I don't see . . . (*She crosses and sits on the divan*)
LARRY. Oh, come now, Miss Byfield. (*He rises and moves to* R *of her*) You know you did. If it hadn't been for what you said that night I should have tried to forget all about it—as if it had been a nasty dream.
HESTER. But—what did I say?
LARRY (*wide-eyed*) Well, you *know* what you said.
HESTER (*almost frantically*) I don't. I don't.
LARRY. Well, don't you remember when you brought me back here and gave me that nice cup of coffee, an' I said I wanted to forget what 'ad 'appened, and I asked you to say nothing about it to nobody, an' *you* said we couldn't 'ush it up; that it was our duty to let everybody know what kind of a man we'd got for a Vicar? You remember that, don't you?
HESTER (*looking at him as if hypnotized*) No. No, I don't. Larry, that isn't true.
LARRY (*blandly*) 'Course it's true. An' you don't remember telling me I ought to tell everything to Mr Granger?
HESTER. It was you who suggested . . .
LARRY. Of course, you *were* very upset that night, p'raps you *don't* remember? I know I should 'ave been upset in your place. You were sweet on him, weren't you, Miss Byfield? (*He crosses to the fireplace*)

(HESTER *winces*)

HESTER (*after running a hand over her brow; wearily*) You said something just now about a meeting and that we had to talk about it.
LARRY (*perkily*) That's right. They want us both there, and . . .

HESTER (*quickly*) Oh, no!
LARRY. Oh, yes. It's only natural. They'll want to know what happened, and we'll have to tell 'em, but of course, we must both tell the same tale. (*He sits in the armchair above the fireplace*)
HESTER. Tale?
LARRY. Well, you know what I mean. I don't mean lies, of course, but—well—you seem so—so funny tonight; seem as if you can't remember nothing; so I just thought we ought to make sure you *do* remember what happened, see? An' it's important that you do remember, otherwise it's only my word against his, see? You're my witness. (*He rises and crosses above the divan to* L *of it*)
HESTER. I can only say what I saw and heard. I've already told Mr Granger. I don't see why I should be made to go to a meeting. I don't want to go. I couldn't face all those people, knowing that they thought I was . . . (*She is almost weeping, but pulls herself together with an effort*) Larry, if I make you a cup of coffee, will you please drink it and then go? (*She rises*) I feel really ill.
LARRY (*crossing to the armchair above the fireplace and sitting*) 'Course I will, but you 'ave a cup, too, then p'raps you'll feel better. I'm sorry you don't feel well, and if I knew where everything was I'd offer to make the coffee myself. Mind you, it wouldn't be as good as yours, Miss Byfield.
HESTER (*hardly listening to him*) I won't be long. (*She collects her empty glass from the table and moves to the arch up* R)
LARRY. Don't you hurry, I'm ever so comfy here. (*He picks up the box of Christmas cards and looks through them*) You've got your Christmas cards, I see.
HESTER (*annoyed, but almost spiritless*) Larry, please, you mustn't . . .
LARRY (*pawing his way through the cards*) Nice, aren't they? Which one are you going to send me, Miss Byfield? You'll 'ave one to spare *now*, won't you?

(HESTER *is about to retort sharply, but thinks better of it and exits up* R. LARRY *looks after her, grins, shoves the cards carelessly back into the box, rises, looks towards the arch up* R *and begins to work his way casually towards the bureau down* L, *humming "Holy Night" quietly as he does so. He stands looking at the bureau for a moment, hesitates and is about to open it.*

HESTER *enters up* R. *She carries a tray of coffee things for two.* LARRY's *hands, which have scarcely touched the lid of the bureau, travel up and pick up the photograph from the top*)

I was just lookin' at this photograph, Miss Byfield. It's you, isn't it?
HESTER (*putting the tray on the coffee table*) Yes. It was taken some years ago.
LARRY. You weren't 'alf a smasher then, weren't you?

HESTER. Be careful how you put it down. The support at the back is broken.
LARRY. Yes, I can see it is. I'll 'ave to mend it for you one of these fine days. (*With his back to her, he replaces the photograph on the bureau*)

(HESTER *moves towards the arch up* R, *stops, looks at Larry, then at the bureau. Her hand goes to her mouth. She quickly controls herself*)

HESTER (*quietly*) The coffee won't be three or four minutes now. But I must stay in the kitchen and keep an eye on the milk.

(HESTER *exits up* R. LARRY *stands for a moment, wipes his brow with his handkerchief, then opens the bureau and looks for the cash-box.*

HESTER, *with extreme caution, re-enters and stands watching Larry.* LARRY *opens the cash-box, takes out the notes, quickly notes how many there are and takes one. He is about to close the lid of the cash-box when he turns and sees Hester watching him. He has the note still in his hand. After a pause he replaces the note in the cash-box. There is a moment of complete stillness as they both look at one another. This is held, then* LARRY *moves slowly away from the bureau to the armchair above the fireplace, and sits.* HESTER *crosses to the bureau, opens the cash-box, counts the notes, then replaces them in the box but does not close either the lid of the cash-box or the bureau. She then crosses to the arch up* R)

LARRY (*leaping up and running towards Hester*) Where are you going?
HESTER (*quietly*) For your coffee.

(HESTER *exits up* R. LARRY *stands, obviously listening to her movements.*

HESTER *re-enters. She carries a pot of coffee and milk mixed, which she puts on the tray.* LARRY, *watching her, sits in the armchair above the fireplace.* HESTER *pours the coffee with trembling hands*)

(*Almost in a whisper*) You take sugar, don't you?
LARRY (*muttering*) Yes. Three. I've got a sweet tooth.

(HESTER *puts some sugar in Larry's cup, then moves* C)

(*He picks up his cup, alert to every move of Hester's, and sips his coffee. With a smirk*) You 'aven't doped it, 'ave you?

(HESTER *does not reply. She stands away from Larry, clutching and unclutching her hands*)

(*He drinks his coffee, still watching her, and puts his cup on the tray*) Well? What are you just standing there like that for—washing your hands? Why don't you say something?
HESTER. Will you please finish your coffee and go.
LARRY. So as you can get on the phone and tell the police that I'm a thief or something? Not bloody likely.

(HESTER *winces but pulls herself together*)

HESTER (*quietly, but with a note of hysteria in her voice*) But you are a thief. I caught you. I saw you with my own eyes. And tonight wasn't the first time, was it?

LARRY. Yes, it was, honest, Miss Byfield.

HESTER (*crossing to the fireplace*) You're lying. You're lying! Last night—you took ten shillings then, didn't you?

LARRY (*smarmingly*) Now listen, Miss Byfield . . . (*He rises*)

HESTER. Answer me. (*With a step towards him*) You took ten shillings from my cash-box last night, didn't you?

LARRY. All right, I did. So what? (*He suddenly grabs her by the wrists*) What are you going to do about it, eh? What are you going to do about it?

HESTER. Let me go. Let me go. I'll call for help.

LARRY. If you was to do that, and I was to shove this cushion —(*he picks up a cushion from the armchair with one hand*) in your face —and keep on shoving . . .

(HESTER *gasps and draws away from him*)

HESTER (*horrified*) What are you saying? What do you . . .?

LARRY (*releasing her and tossing the cushion on to the chair; laughing quietly*) I thought that'd put the wind up you.

(HESTER *retreats to the fireplace*)

You didn't think I meant it, did you? I just wanted to stop you from behavin' like a silly old woman. (*He picks up the cushion*) 'Course, if you *won't* stop behavin' like one . . . (*He tosses the cushion into the air and catches it as it comes down*) Well then, of course, we'll 'ave to see. (*He replaces the cushion on the chair*) Won't we? Wouldn't it be awful if I 'ad to? (*He lights a cigarette*) What're you thinking about? (*He moves in front of the armchair, puts his foot up and sits on the left arm*)

HESTER. I'm thinking about—how you have fooled me—everyone. I'm thinking of you as you are now, and as you were when I first knew you; when I taught you in Sunday School.

LARRY (*laughing*) I was your favourite, wasn't I, Miss Byfield? I'll say I was. Couldn't keep your hands off my bare knees, could you?

HESTER (*crossing down* L) Oh—God! Get out of my house. Get out. You're loathsome—foul. You ought to be horsewhipped, and if it's in my power I'll see that you are. (*She crosses to* L *of him*) I'll see Mr Granger. I'll tell him what I've found out about you. (*Almost shouting*) Yes, and that I believe your accusation against the Vicar is nothing more than a filthy deliberate lie.

LARRY (*jumping up*) By God, but you won't.

HESTER (*shouting*) It is a lie, isn't it? And you've made me a party to it. You deliberately made me believe . . .

LARRY (*shouting her down*) "Made you." There wasn't no

making about it. You believed it because you wanted to believe it. You jumped at it. You wasn't thinking about me when you said I ought to tell Mr Granger.

HESTER. Of course I was. What else . . .? (*She sits on the end of the divan*)

LARRY. Don't try to come it with me. It won't wash. All you was thinking was what a fine chance this would be to pay the Vicar out for . . .

HESTER (*faltering*) Why should I want to pay him out, as you call it? For what? What had he done to me?

LARRY. Nothing, when you come to think of it. It wasn't what he'd done. It was what *you'd* done. Made yourself the laughing stock of the village. (*He crosses above the divan and stands up* L)

HESTER. What?

LARRY. Good Lord! There wasn't a kid of six in the place who couldn't see you was after him. Flung yourself at him, didn't you? (*He moves down* C) Couldn't shove his nose out of the door but you was after him. You should 'ave 'eard what they said about you in the village. "There she goes. Barmy Byfield's after her man again." That's what they used to say. "After him, she is, like a dog after a . . ." (*He roars with laughter*)

(HESTER *rises and crosses to the fireplace*)

(*He moves to* L *of her*) But you didn't get 'im, did you? He didn't want you, did he? And you *knew* he didn't, and that's why you was so damn glad when I gave you the chance to 'ave your own back on him. You hate him like poison. And so do I. He's had it in for me ever since he came in the village, but by God he's going to pay for it now. An' if you keep your mouth shut we'll 'ave 'im out of this place a damn sight faster than he came in. And you're goin' to keep your mouth shut, aren't you? (*He picks up the cushion*) 'Cos if you aren't I'll 'ave to shut it for you.

(HESTER *sways, then almost collapses into the armchair down* R, *sobbing*)

Here, chuck it, chuck it. (*He replaces the cushion*) Crying isn't goin' to get us nowhere, is it? (*He turns away up* C)

HESTER. Go away, please go away. Can't you see I'm ill? Larry, please leave me.

LARRY. I'm not leaving till you promise to keep your mouth shut about me pinchin' your money, and about me an' the Vicar, see? An' it's for your own good, isn't it, Miss Byfield? I mean to say, you'll look such a bloody fool, won't you, if it comes out that you egged me on to say the Vicar tried to mess about with me, just 'cos you wanted to get your own back on him 'cos he wouldn't fall for your maidenly charms?

(HESTER *rises quickly and rushes wildly at Larry as if to strike him. After a very brief struggle,* LARRY *throws her back on to the divan. She lies back, panting*)

Now don't be silly, Miss Byfield. I don't want to hurt a pretty woman like you.

(HESTER *suddenly leans back, quite still, with her eyes closed*)

(*He moves to* R *of the divan*) Here—what the . . .? Come on, Miss Byfield. Pull yourself together for God's sake. You're all right, aren't you? (*He bends over her*) Come on, now.

HESTER. Please get me some water.

(LARRY *exits up* R. HESTER *rises quickly, moves to the bureau and lifts the telephone receiver*)

(*Into the telephone. Breathlessly*) Three-four-two, please . . . Hallo? . . . Three-four-two? . . . Vicar, this is Hester Byfield. I must speak to you . . .

(LARRY *enters up* R. *He carries a glass of water. The moment he sees Hester with the receiver in her hand, he almost throws the glass to the floor and rushes at Hester*)

LARRY. You cunning . . . (*He drags her* C *and throws her on to the divan*)

(HESTER *screams. She is still clutching the receiver, so that the telephone falls to the floor*)

Who was you ringing up, eh? Who was it? If you don't tell me I'll knock the livin' daylight out of you.

HESTER (*weakly*) I didn't get through.

(LARRY *picks up the telephone, takes the receiver from Hester, listens for a moment, then replaces the receiver, leaving the telephone on the floor*)

LARRY. Who were you going to ring up?
HESTER. I didn't get through.

(*The telephone rings.* LARRY *looks at Hester for a moment, lifts the receiver, quickly slams his hand on the receiver rest and puts the receiver on the floor*)

LARRY (*livid*) Didn't get through, eh. Didn't get through. You lying old . . . (*He lands out at Hester*)

(HESTER *manages to evade the blow*)

HESTER (*running to the fireplace; screaming*) No. Larry. No! (*She grabs the scissors from the mantelpiece and turns to face Larry*)
LARRY (*about to rush at Hester*) What you got there?
HESTER (*sobbing*) Keep away. (*She moves above the armchair towards the door up* C)

ACT III   SERIOUS CHARGE   65

LARRY. Now look, Miss Byfield . . . (*He rushes up* C *and stands between Hester and the door*)
HESTER. Keep away. (*She backs down* L *of the divan*)
LARRY. Put them down. D'y' hear? Put them scissors down. You'll hurt yourself.
HESTER. If you come near me . . .
LARRY. Now don't be silly. Put them scissors down. We don't want no accidents. Here! Give 'em to me.

(LARRY *moves to* HESTER, *they struggle for a moment, then* LARRY *breaks away, with a little yell, holding his hand. The jerk makes* HESTER *pull the scissors violently to her. She gives a scream and stands clutching her breast. The scissors fall to the floor*)

(*In horror*) Oh, God! (*He moves towards Hester*)
HESTER (*staggering towards the steps of the bedroom door*) Keep away!
LARRY (*stopping; terrified*) Miss Byfield.
HESTER (*sobbing as she drags herself up the steps*) Keep away.

(HESTER, *with a supreme effort, exits through the bedroom door. The door slams behind her and the key is heard turning in the lock. There is a tiny pause, then a thud.* HESTER *has fallen to the floor immediately behind the bedroom door*)

LARRY (*hearing the thud*) Miss Byfield! (*He rushes to the bedroom door and tries to open it*) Miss Byfield! (*He hammers on the door*) Miss Byfield, let me in. Let me in for God's sake. (*He hammers on the door*) Speak to me then—if you won't open the door, speak to me. Tell me you're all right. (*He listens. Except for his own panting there is silence. He backs away from the door and, almost blubbering, mutters to himself*) She did it. It wasn't me. (*He breaks down completely*) Oh, God! Oh, God! (*He looks wildly around*) I've got to get out of here.

(*The voices of men singing carols are heard approaching*)

(*He hears the voices*) Oh, God! (*He runs up* C, *switches out the lights and is about to exit*)

(*The sound of a car arriving and stopping is heard off*)

VOICES (*off; overlapping each other*) Jim, look! It's 'im. It's parson. Stand clear, lads. Take that, you son of a . . .

(*There is a crash of glass off*)

Gord! Right through 'is windscreen. Here he is. Let 'im 'ave it, lads.

(*The noise now becomes confusion.* LARRY, *during this, and now in complete panic, hides in the corner up* L. *There is a sharp rap on the door knocker and the door opens immediately.*

HOWARD *comes quickly into the room, closing the door behind* him. *Stones can be heard hitting the door, and there are more shouts and yells*)

HOWARD. Miss Byfield, I'm sorry to . . . (*He stops, looks around the room but does not see Larry, moves down* R *of the divan and calls*) Miss Byfield!

(*There is a long silence*)

(*He crosses to* LC, *catches his foot on the telephone, looks at it for a moment, but does not touch it. He then moves towards the corner where Larry is in the shadow*) Who's that? Miss Byfield, is that you? (*He takes an electric torch from his pocket and switches it on*)

(LARRY *is seen in the light of the torch.* HOWARD *gives a gasp, but does not speak.* LARRY, *too, is silent. This situation is held for quite a time*)

(*In a cold voice*) Where is Miss Byfield?
LARRY. Listen, Vicar, I . . .
HOWARD (*cutting in*) Where is Miss Byfield?
LARRY (*after a pause*) I—I don't know. She isn't here.
HOWARD. Then what are you doing he——? (*Quickly*) Never mind. Just stay where you are. (*He switches off his torch, moves to the front door, switches on the lights and steps into the doorway*)

(*The shouts off begin again*)

(*He calls*) Johnson! And one of you others—Roberts. Come here. (*He stands* L *of the doorway*)

(*More shouts are heard off*)

(*He yells*) You damned idiots, shut up!

(*The noise quietens a little*)

Johnson! Roberts! Do as I tell you. Come here.

(*The shouting now becomes a subdued murmur.*
    JOHNSON *and* ROBERTS, *two villagers, appear in the doorway*)

JOHNSON. Here! What's the . . .? (*He comes into the room*)
HOWARD (*cutting in*) Slip across to the school-house. Ask Mr Granger to come across here right away.
JOHNSON. But what . . .?
HOWARD (*overlapping*) Do as I tell you. Tell him it's urgent.

(JOHNSON, *after a second's pause, exits by the front door*)

Roberts! You come in here.
ROBERTS (*coming into the room*) What's the game, eh?
HOWARD (*curtly*) Shut that door, and stay where you are.

(ROBERTS *closes the door and stands, wonderingly, by it.* HOWARD *crosses to the fireplace*)

LARRY (*moving to* L *of the divan*) Vicar, listen, I . . .
ROBERTS (*seeing Larry*) What . . .? Larry?
HOWARD (*firmly*) You will tell me nothing. Whatever you have to say, you can say to Mr Granger.
LARRY. But . . .
HOWARD. Shut up! Don't let him out of this room, Roberts. (*He crosses and looks down at the telephone*)
ROBERTS (*awed but curious*) What's up, Larry?

(LARRY, *watching Howard, does not reply.* HOWARD *looks from the telephone to Larry, looks around the room and sees the scissors on the floor. He shows no interest in these, but* LARRY, *when he sees Howard looking at them, gives a little gasp.* HOWARD *then turns, looks at Larry, then again at the scissors, then Larry again. He moves to the bureau, looks at the open cash-box, then moves to the steps of the bedroom door.* LARRY *involuntarily moves forward.* HOWARD *stops with one foot on the first step.* LARRY *sinks on to the divan and covers his face with his hands. There is a very definite pause, broken by a knock at the front door*)

(*To Howard. Quietly*) Shall I open it?
HOWARD. Yes.

(ROBERTS *opens the front door.*
GRANGER *enters by the front door*)

GRANGER (*as he enters*) What's going on here? Where . . .? (*He moves down* R) Oh, there you are, Vicar. I understand you want me.
HOWARD. Yes, I do.
GRANGER. What is it? What's Roberts doing here?
HOWARD. All right, Roberts. You can go.
ROBERTS. What?
HOWARD. Get back to your friends outside. Tell them I shan't be long—if they want to have another go at me. (*He moves up* L)
ROBERTS. But—Vicar . . .
HOWARD (*suddenly and furiously*) Get out. (*He puts his hand to his head*) I'm sorry. (*Very quietly*) Please—go.

(ROBERTS, *after a look at them all, exits by the front door*)

GRANGER. Now what is all this, Phillips?
LARRY (*rising and running to Granger*) Mr Granger, you've got to listen to me.
GRANGER (*brushing Larry aside*) Just a moment. (*To Howard*) What's he doing here?
HOWARD. You'd better ask him.
GRANGER (*moving up* C) I'd rather hear what you have to say first.
HOWARD. You would? How surprising, Granger.
GRANGER. Phillips, please.

HOWARD. Very well, these are the facts. About ten minutes ago, Miss Byfield rang me up. All she said was, "I must speak to you . . ." Then I heard a crash. She screamed. I decided to come over here. When I arrived I was attacked by that gang out there. I came in here. He was alone in the room. I asked him where Miss Byfield was. He said she wasn't here.

GRANGER (*after glancing round the room*) Larry, what's been going on here? (*He moves to R of the divan*)

LARRY (*mumbling*) I—I don't know. It's nothing to do with me.

(GRANGER *gives Larry a long, doubting look*)

GRANGER (*to Howard*) You say Miss Byfield isn't in the house? (*He moves to the arch up R and looks off*)

HOWARD. I didn't say so; he did.

GRANGER (*moving C; sharply*) But haven't you looked to see?

HOWARD (*turning and looking straight at Granger*) No, I haven't.

GRANGER. Why not?

HOWARD. He said she wasn't here.

GRANGER. You—you mean to say you took his word for that?

HOWARD. Don't you?

GRANGER. No, I'm damned if I do. There's something fishy about all this.

HOWARD (*looking at Granger in wonderment*) Granger—you don't take his word—now—and yet . . .

GRANGER (*turning on Larry*) Larry, where is Miss Byfield?

LARRY (*sobbing*) Mr Granger, you've got to believe me.

GRANGER (*grabbing him by the lapels*) Where is Miss Byfield?

LARRY. She's—she's . . . (*He breaks down completely*) I didn't do it. I didn't do it. She did it herself.

GRANGER. Did what? For God's sake, boy, pull yourself together.

LARRY (*pointing to the scissors on the floor down L*) She grabbed hold of the scissors . . .

GRANGER. *What?*

LARRY. I was trying to get them away from her—it was an accident . . .

GRANGER (*frantically*) Damn you, boy. Where *is* she?

LARRY (*pointing to the bedroom door*) Up there. She's up there—but the door—I can't open it. (*He falls on to the divan and sobs*)

(GRANGER *crosses quickly to the bedroom door and tries to open it*)

GRANGER (*shouting*) Miss Byfield! Miss Byfield! (*He tries the door*) Phillips, I can't get this damned door open. Pass me a poker or something. Hurry.

HOWARD (*moving to the front door*) I'll get in through the window—it'll be quicker.

(HOWARD *exits by the front door*)

GRANGER (*crossing to* R *of the divan*) Here! You'd better pull yourself together and tell me what's been going on in this house tonight.
LARRY. It *was* an accident, Mr Granger. I swear it was.
GRANGER. What were you doing here?
LARRY. I—I—came to see Miss Byfield.
GRANGER. Had she asked you to call on her?
LARRY. No—I—I . . . (*He breaks down again*)
GRANGER. Then why did you?

(MRS PHILLIPS *enters by the front door*)

Answer me.
MRS PHILLIPS. Mr Granger—Howard, he is here, isn't he? (*She moves to* L *of the divan*)
GRANGER. Yes, Mrs Phillips. He's—we're not sure, but I'm afraid something terrible has happened.
MRS PHILLIPS. Hester—Miss Byfield . . .
GRANGER. Yes. We can't get this door open. (*He moves impatiently towards the bedroom door. As he does so he sees the open cash-box. He starts, moves to the bureau, picks up the cash-box and turns to Larry. Quietly*) Good God! Was it . . .? Was *this* why you came? Is this why you were struggling with her?
LARRY (*leaping up*) I didn't take any of the money. I swear I didn't.
GRANGER (*replacing the cash-box and crossing to Larry*) Then why were you struggling with her? Answer me, damn you.
LARRY. She was trying to get out of the house.
GRANGER. And you were trying to stop her?
LARRY. Yes.
GRANGER. Why?
LARRY. I—I . . .
GRANGER. Why were you trying to stop her from leaving the house?

(LARRY *can only blubber*)

(*Firmly*) Larry! God knows what has happened here tonight, but do you realize that if anything has happened to Miss Byfield—if she's dead—you will have to stand trial for murder.
LARRY (*wildly*) But I didn't do it. It was an accident.
GRANGER. If it was you'll have to prove it. And it will be no use you telling lies or refusing to answer questions, so you may as well begin by telling the truth now. Why was Miss Byfield trying to get out of this house, and why were you trying to stop her?
LARRY (*after a slight pause; his hand to his head*) She—she was going to see you—and the Vicar . . .
GRANGER. Why?

LARRY. She was going to tell you that—that . . . (*He looks at Mrs Phillips*)
GRANGER. Well, go on. Tell us what?
LARRY. That what I'd said about the Vicar—wasn't true.
GRANGER. *What?*

(MRS PHILLIPS *crosses to the fireplace*)

LARRY (*mumbling*) That it was all lies.
GRANGER. Oh, my God! (*He grips Larry and almost shakes him*) And *was* it? Was it all lies?
LARRY (*hysterically*) Yes. (*He sobs*)
GRANGER (*looking at Larry; slowly*) You filthy, despicable little swine.

(*The bedroom door opens and* HOWARD *appears in the doorway. He stands there motionless*)

MRS PHILLIPS. Howard! (*She moves* RC)

(GRANGER *turns to look at Howard*)

LARRY (*almost in a whisper*) Is she—dead? Is she . . .?

(HOWARD *does not answer, but stands looking at Larry*)

MRS PHILLIPS (*aghast*) Howard, she isn't . . .?

(MRS PHILLIPS *crosses quickly to the bedroom door and exits.*
GRANGER, *after a second's pause, follows Mrs Phillips off.*
HOWARD *closes the door behind them, and comes slowly down into the room, his eyes still fixed on Larry*)

LARRY (*his eyes on Howard*) She *is* dead, isn't she? I know she is.

(HOWARD, *after a slight pause, picks up the telephone and puts the receiver on the rest*)

(*He moves to Howard*) Don't get the police—not yet. Give me a chance to tell you what happened.

(HOWARD *puts the telephone on the bureau, then crosses to the fireplace*)

(*He crosses to* RC) I tell you she grabbed them scissors and I tried to get them away from her. She did it herself. She did, Mr Phillips, I swear she did.
HOWARD. Don't waste your breath trying to convince me.
LARRY (*wildly*) But I've got to make you believe me.
HOWARD (*turning on him*) You young fool! What does it matter whether I believe you or not?
LARRY. But, Mr Phillips . . .
HOWARD. What I believe doesn't matter any more. You've seen to that, haven't you? (*He turns to the fireplace*)

LARRY. But you're the Vicar—if you told them—if you told the police they will listen to you.

HOWARD (*turning*) They might have done, Larry. But not now. You stupid fool. Don't you understand that as a decent citizen—as a man whose word is respected—I'm finished? Thanks to you.

LARRY. But I'll tell everybody I lied about the other night. That I made it all up.

HOWARD. You're a bit late for that, aren't you?

LARRY. I've told Mr Granger. I've told him I was lying. I'll tell everybody, honest I will.

HOWARD. You've made a bad move there, Larry. You shouldn't have told Mr Granger.

LARRY. I don't know what you're talking about.

HOWARD. You should have stuck to your lies, and gone on telling them. Do you seriously believe that anyone is going to believe that you lied about *me*, but that you're telling the truth about Miss Byfield?

LARRY. I am. I am.

HOWARD. Isn't it common sense that if you lied about one thing you'd lie about another—especially if you're trying to save your own miserable neck?

LARRY (*wildly*) Oh, God! Oh, God! What am I going to do? (*He crosses to the divan, sinks on it and weeps*)

HOWARD. Perhaps you are telling the truth, Larry—about Miss Byfield—but I doubt if anyone's going to believe you.

(LARRY *buries his face in his hands, hopelessly.* HOWARD *stands watching him for a while, expressing no feeling of any kind.*

MRS PHILLIPS *enters from the bedroom, moves to the telephone and lifts the receiver*)

MRS PHILLIPS (*into the telephone*) Four-two-eight, please . . .

(HOWARD *stands at the fireplace with his back to the room.*

GRANGER *enters from the bedroom, crosses and stands up* R)

Is that Doctor Richards' house? . . . Is the doctor in? . . . Oh . . . Well, when he comes in would you ask him to call at Miss Byfield's? . . . There's been an accident . . . No, not really. Just a cut and she is rather shaken . . . Thank you . . . Mrs Phillips, from the Vicarage . . . Thank you. (*She replaces the receiver*)

LARRY (*at first unable to believe*) She—she isn't . . . (*He turns slowly to Howard. When he speaks his voice is high-pitched, almost hysterical*) You—bastard! (*He breaks down completely*)

GRANGER (*moving to Larry*) Get out. You'll go to that meeting tomorrow night.

(LARRY *stops and turns up* C)

You're going to stand up in front of the Church Council—in front of the whole village if necessary, and tell them that the filthy accusation you made against the Vicar, you made deliberately, knowing it to be nothing but a pack of lies. You'll stand up and tell them that——

(LARRY *makes a half move of protest*)

—or you'll hear a Magistrate tell you it in Court.

(LARRY, *with his eyes on Howard, moves to the front door*)

Get out!

(LARRY *exits slowly by the front door*)

(*He closes the door, then turns and moves down* RC) Phillips—I—(*hesitantly*) I know that words are easy—convenient—but I ask you in all humility, to forgive me. (*He holds out his hand*)

(HOWARD, *after a moment, turns, looks at Granger, then turns away again.* MRS PHILLIPS *moves up* L)

I'm sorry.
HOWARD. So am I.
GRANGER. Don't think I don't understand.
HOWARD. You don't, Granger. You can't. Oh, God! What has that boy done to me? He's done more than turn this village against me. He's . . .
GRANGER. But you don't suppose that anyone will believe, now, that . . .
HOWARD. No, not now—but what does it matter whether the village believes in me or not—what anyone believes—when I can't believe in myself?
GRANGER. What do you mean?
HOWARD. I mean, Granger, that I'm not fit to hold my job. (*He pauses briefly*) I can't forgive, Granger. "Forgive us our trespasses as we forgive them that . . ." (*He shakes his head*) And yet I can't take your hand. I can't go up there—(*he nods towards the bedroom door*) and say a few words of comfort and assurance to Hester Byfield. I can't forget—stones crashing through my windows; obscene letters shoved through the letter-box; the disbelief and contemptuous loathing on the faces of my own parishioners. (*He pauses slightly and crosses slowly to* C) I *see* all that, Granger, and what I *feel* is a deadly hatred that has grown up inside me. I've tried to fight it. From the first I've tried to say—as He did—"Father, forgive them, for they know not what they do", but the words choked in my throat, and I gave myself up to hatred—a hatred so deep that I could make that boy suffer as I did just now. I led him to believe that Hester Byfield was dead, when all the time I knew she was in no danger. I watched his agony, Granger, and I gloated over it. I, a preacher of God's Gospel, did that—deliberately.

ACT III SERIOUS CHARGE 73

GRANGER. In your place, I'm not sure I shouldn't have done the same.

HOWARD (*moving down* LC *and turning to face Granger*) But you are *not* in my place. No man can put himself in another's place. Can you honestly condone what I did, Granger? No, of course you can't. Why am I wearing this cloth? What is my purpose in this village? Why do I go into the pulpit every Sunday if not to preach the greatest of all Christian truths—that forgiveness is everything? And here I am, faced with the fact that not only can I not forgive, but what's more—and what's worse—that I don't want to. (*He pauses*) I must get out of the Church—or at any rate, out of this place; work out my salvation elsewhere. (*He moves down* L)

GRANGER (*moving* C; *after a pause*) You're a merciless judge, Phillips. You put yourself in the dock, prosecute yourself and find yourself guilty of being unfit for your job without giving the jury a chance to consider their verdict. Won't you let us—the village —decide whether you're fit for your job or not? God knows we don't deserve it, but give us the chance to make up to you in some small measure, for the wrong we've done you. We need you here among us, Vicar. If you stay, we can try to redeem ourselves, not only in your eyes, but our own as well.

HOWARD. Everyone striving to make my life a bed of roses for me? You think that's the answer? (*He crosses and sits on the downstage end of the divan*)

MRS PHILLIPS (*after a pause*) Your life won't be a bed of roses. Mr Granger speaks glibly—forgive me, Mr Granger—of "we, the village". But I don't believe that *everyone* in the village will bow their heads in shame because they believed what they did of you. I don't believe *everyone's* going to *stop* believing what they did. What has happened tonight may well restore the confidence of those who have always wanted to believe in you, but what about the others who don't? Who don't because it's so much more fun not to believe? It's amongst all these, Howard, that you must work out your salvation. Mr Granger says that "we, the village" need you. (*She shrugs her shoulders*) That may be—I don't know. But I do know that there is *one* who needs you—needs you as much as you need him—that boy. Can't you see, Howard, if you leave this place now, if you desert him when every God-fearing person in the village will be against him, then he's lost for ever. (*She pauses*) You must stay. You must try to understand the evil that is in the boy, and fight to help him conquer it, even hating him as you do. No matter whether you win or lose, the fight will restore in *you* the faith in yourself that you've lost—and so badly need.

(*There is a knock at the front door*)

(*Very quietly*) That may be the doctor. (*She goes to the front door and opens it*)

(EVA *is revealed standing outside the front door*)

(*Surprised. Quietly*) Eva!
EVA. Is the Vicar here, ma'am?
MRS PHILLIPS. Yes. Come in, Eva.

(EVA *comes into the room.* MRS PHILLIPS *shuts the door*)

EVA (*moving to* L *of Howard; quietly*) I've been looking for you, sir. I saw your car outside.
MRS PHILLIPS (*crossing to the chair down* L *and sitting*) What is it, Eva?
EVA. Old Mrs White, ma'am.
MRS PHILLIPS. What's the matter with her?
EVA. I've been up there looking after her—since I left the Vicarage. She was taken real bad tonight. The doctor's with her. He thinks it's the end this time. (*To Howard*) She's asking for you, sir.
HOWARD (*very quietly*) Thank you, Eva, for letting me know.
EVA (*to Mrs Phillips; with a little outburst*) And, ma'am, you *will* let me come back to the Vicarage, won't you? I don't care what they say about the Vicar, I know it's all a lot of lies.

(MRS PHILLIPS *looks towards* HOWARD, *who looks at* EVA. MRS PHILLIPS *takes Eva's hand in gratitude*)

MRS PHILLIPS (*looking at Howard, but speaking quietly to Eva*) We want you back with us—(*to Howard*) so much.
HOWARD (*after a moment; to Eva*) Did the doctor say how long it will be, Eva?
EVA. He says she won't live through the night, sir.

(HOWARD *rises and moves to the front door*)

HOWARD (*stopping and turning*) Don't wait up for me, Mother. I shall stay—till the end.

(HOWARD *exits by the front door.* MRS PHILLIPS *and* GRANGER *exchange little smiles as—*

the CURTAIN *falls*

FURNITURE AND PROPERTY PLOT

ACT I

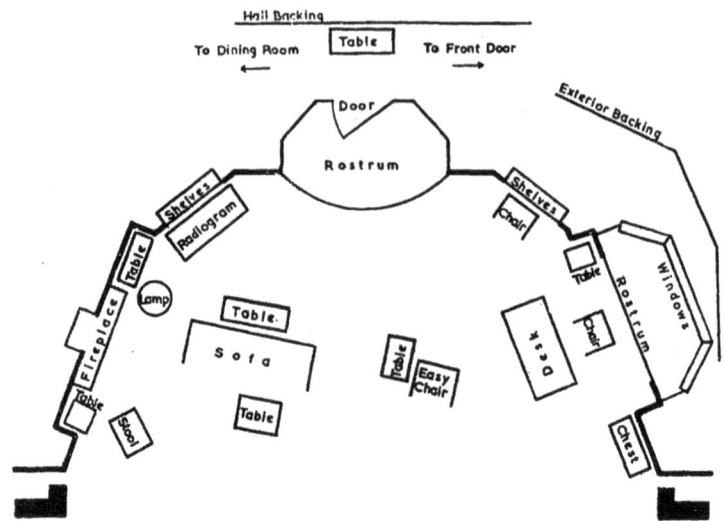

Scene 1

On stage—Occasional table (down R). *On it:* box with cigarettes, table lighter, ashtray, box of matches, ornament
Occasional table (R). *On it:* vase
Radiogram. *In it:* records
Table (behind sofa). *On it:* tray, soda syphon, decanter of sherry, decanter of whisky, 3 whisky glasses, 3 sherry glasses
Sofa. *On it:* cushions
Low coffee table
Occasional table (LC)
Easy chair. *On it:* cushion
Upright chair
Desk chair
Desk. *On it:* telephone, box with cigarettes, pipe-stand with pipes, matches, pen-stand, pens, inkwell, miscellaneous papers, envelopes, writing paper, engagement diary, scribbling pad, pencil, tobacco jar with tobacco, Howard's pipe, filled, blotter, ashtray, table-lamp
Occasional table (up L). *On it:* vase of flowers
Waste-paper basket
Low chest. *On it:* magazines, ornament
Standard lamp
Built-in bookshelves. *On them:* books, busts
On mantelpiece: photograph, ashtray, vases, clock, prop vase for breaking

　　　　　　Fireside stool
　　　　　　Fender
　　　　　　Fire-irons
　　　　　　Fire-grate
　　　　　　Fire-screen
　　　　　　Hearth-brush
　　　　　　Hearth-rug
　　　　　　Over fireplace: mirror
　　　　　　Carpet on floor
　　　　　　Runner LC
　　　　　　Pictures on walls
　　　　　　Light switches R of door
　　　　　　4 pairs electric-candle wall-brackets
　　　　　　Heavy window curtains
　　　　　　Pelmet
　　　　　　In hall: table. *On it:* silver salver with folded evening paper
Off stage—Silver tray. *On it:* cloth, pot with coffee, jug of milk, basin of sugar,
　　　　　　　　2 each coffee-cups, saucers and spoons (EVA)
　　　　　　2 books, newspaper (HOWARD)
　　　　　　Tray. *On it:* cloth, bowl of soup, soup spoon, roll and butter on plate,
　　　　　　　　knife, cruet, table napkin in ring (EVA)
　　　　　　Mrs Phillips' cape (HOWARD)
Personal—HESTER: handbag. *In it:* handkerchief
Window curtains closed
Door closed
Wall-brackets on
Fire on
Standard lamp out
Table-lamp out

　　　　　　　　　　SCENE 2

Strike—Used glasses
　　　　　　Books and newspaper from desk
　　　　　　Firescreen
　　　　　　Flowers from table up L
Set—*On table up* L: vase of Autumn leaves
　　　　On easy chair: knitting bag with knitting
　　　　On floor by easy chair: ball of wool
Window curtains closed
Door closed
Wall-brackets on
Fire on
Standard lamp on
Table-lamp on
Personal—HOWARD: pipe, pouch with tobacco, matches
　　　　　　HESTER: watch, new handbag. *In it:* cigarette case with cigarettes,
　　　　　　　　　　　　brooch in box, Dunhill pipe in box
　　　　　　MARY: handkerchief

　　　　　　　　　　ACT II
　　　　　　　　　　SCENE 1

Strike—Wrapping and gift boxes
　　　　　　Dirty glasses
　　　　　　Knitting
Set—*On desk:* Dunhill pipe
Replace ashtray on table down R

SERIOUS CHARGE

Window curtains closed
Door open
Wall-brackets on
Fire on
Standard lamp off
Table-lamp off

Personal—HOWARD: watch, pipe, pouch with tobacco, matches
    HESTER: gloves, handbag
    LARRY: packet of cigarettes, matches

SCENE 2

Strike—Broken ornaments
    Standard lamp shade

Replace books in shelves
Replace articles on desk

Set—New ornaments on mantelpiece
    Patched shade on standard lamp

Window curtains closed
Door closed
Wall-brackets on
Fire on
Standard lamp off
Table-lamp off

Off stage—Newspaper (HOWARD)
    Tray. *On it:* tray cloth, pot of tea, 2 cups, 2 saucers, 2 teaspoons, 2 small plates, plate of cakes, jug of milk, basin of sugar (EVA)
    Salver. *On it:* letter (EVA)
    Stone wrapped in paper

Personal—EVA: Handkerchief
    GRANGER: pipe (filled), matches

ACT III

On stage—Divan. *On it:* cushion
    2 wing armchairs. *On them:* cushions
    Low table. *On it:* glass of milk, nearly empty, box of Christmas cards tied with string, list

Table (up LC). *On it:* vase of Autumn leaves, ornaments, photographs
Standard lamp
Bureau. *On it:* telephone, envelopes, bill, pen, inkstand, photograph of Hester in silver frame, cash-box with 5 £1 notes
2 upright chairs
Fender
Fire-grate
Fire-irons
Coal scuttle
Trivet with copper kettle
On mantelpiece: clock, ornaments, Christmas cards, pair of scissors, ashtray
2 wall-brackets
Pendant lamp
Hearth-rug
Small carpet
Chintz window curtains
On walls: horse brasses, warming-pan, pictures, ornamental plates, bellows

Front door bolted
Bedroom door closed
Window closed
Window curtains closed
Wall-brackets lit
Standard lamp lit
Pendant lamp lit

Off stage—Tray. *On it:* cloth, 2 cups, 2 saucers, 2 teaspoons, bowl of sugar (HESTER)
Pot of coffee and milk mixed (HESTER)
Glass of water (LARRY)

Personal—HESTER: handkerchief
LARRY: packet of cigarettes, matches, handkerchief
HOWARD: torch

LIGHTING PLOT

Property Fittings Required—ACTS I and II—4 pairs electric-candle wall-brackets, standard lamp, table-lamp, fire (all practical), light switches R of door up C
    ACT III—2 wall-brackets, standard lamp, pendant lamp, fire (all practical), light switch R of door up C

ACT I SCENE 1 A Living-room. Night

THE APPARENT SOURCES OF LIGHT ARE—wall-brackets up C, wall-brackets R, a standard lamp R, and a table-lamp, L
THE MAIN ACTING AREAS ARE—at a desk L, an easy chair LC, down R, C and at a sofa RC

To open: Lights at ¾
    Strips R and L outside door up C, on
    Blue flood outside window L
    Fire on
    Wall-brackets on
    Standard lamp off
    Table-lamp off

Cue 1 MRS PHILLIPS switches on table-lamp   (page 1)
    Snap in table-lamp
    Bring up lights L to full

Cue 2 MRS PHILLIPS switches on standard lamp   (page 1)
    Snap in standard lamp
    Bring up lights R to full

Cue 3 EVA switches off standard lamp   (page 13)
    Snap out standard lamp
    Reduce lights R to ¾

Cue 4 EVA switches off table-lamp   (page 13)
    Snap out table-lamp
    Reduce lights L to ¾

ACT I SCENE 2 Night

To open: Lights full up
    Strips R and L outside door up C, on
    Blue flood outside window
    Fire on
    Wall-brackets on
    Standard lamp on
    Table-lamp on

No cues

ACT II SCENE 1 Night

To open: Lights at ¾
    Strips R and L outside door up C, on
    Blue flood outside window
    Fire on
    Wall-brackets on
    Standard lamp out
    Table-lamp out

No cues

ACT II SCENE 2 Night

To open: Lights at ¾
   Strips R and L outside door up C, on
   Blue flood outside window
   Fire on
   Wall-brackets on
   Standard lamp out
   Table lamp out

Cue 5 MRS PHILLIPS switches on standard lamp (page 41)
   Snap in standard lamp
   Bring up lights R. to full

ACT III A cottage living-room. Night
  THE APPARENT SOURCES OF LIGHT ARE—wall-brackets R, a standard lamp up L and a pendant lamp C
  THE MAIN ACTING AREAS COVER—the whole stage

To open: Lights full up
   Strips outside door L and arch R
   Blue flood outside door and window back C
   Fire on
   Wall-brackets on
   Standard lamp on
   Pendant lamp on

Cue 6 HESTER switches off lights (page 56)
   Snap out wall-brackets
   Snap out standard lamp
   Snap out pendant lamp
   Snap out onstage lights

Cue 7 HESTER switches on lights (page 57)
   Snap in wall-brackets
   Snap in standard lamp
   Snap in pendant lamp
   Snap in onstage lights

Cue 8 LARRY switches off lights (page 65)
   Snap out wall-brackets
   Snap out standard lamp
   Snap out pendant lamp
   Snap out onstage lights

Cue 9 HOWARD switches on lights (page 66)
   Snap in wall-brackets
   Snap in standard lamp
   Snap in pendant lamp
   Snap in onstage lights

www.ingramcontent.com/pod-product-compliance
Ingram Content Group UK Ltd.
Pitfield, Milton Keynes, MK11 3LW, UK
UKHW021845210426
5322IPUK00022B/468